EVEN FROM
A BROKEN
WEB

EVEN FROM A BROKEN WEB

BRIEF, RESPECTFUL SOLUTION-ORIENTED THERAPY FOR SEXUAL ABUSE AND TRAUMA

Bill O'Hanlon

AND

Bob Bertolino

JOHN WILEY & SONS, INC.

New York • Chichester • Weinheim • Brisbane • Singapore • Toronto

Copyright © 1998 by John Wiley & Sons, Inc. All rights reserved.

Published simultaneously in Canada.

This publication is designed to provide accurate and authoritative information in regard to the subject matter covered. It is sold with the understanding that the publisher is not engaged in rendering legal, accounting, or other professional services. If legal advice or other expert assistance is required, the services of a competent professional person should be sought.

Library of Congress Cataloging-in-Publication Data:

O'Hanlon, Bill, 1952–
    Even from a broken web : brief, respectful solution-oriented
therapy for sexual abuse and trauma / by Bill O'Hanlon, Bob
Bertolino.
        p. cm.
    Includes bibliographical referencs and index.
    ISBN 0-471-19403-4 (cloth : alk. paper)
    1. Sexual abuse victims—Rehabilitation. 2. Solution-focused
therapy. I. Bertolino, Bob, 1965– . II. Title.
RC560.S44059   1998
616.85'83—dc21   97-35488

Printed in the United States of America.

10 9 8 7 6 5 4 3 2 1

To Steffanie, for her love, friendship, and devotion.
To Patrick, for sticking with me through the rough times.
To Mary, without whom I wouldn't have been able to write this.

Bill

To Christine, for making my life complete.
To my mother, Helen Bertolino, for always believing in
possibilities and providing inspiration
in too many ways to mention.
To my father and stepmother,
Tony and Dottie Bertolino, for their support.
To my entire family, especially my brothers and sisters, Mary,
Anita, Tom, Marc, Mike, Andy, and their spouses and children.
There is no way to express how much you all mean to me.
And to Gary: You have brought so much happiness
and love to my life.
I will always treasure that.

Bob

PREFACE

*T*he approach detailed in this book is based in part upon solution-oriented therapy, an approach Bill codeveloped. The idea of solution-oriented therapy is that people do better when we notice and highlight what they do well and how they cope, rather than focus on what they do poorly and how they don't cope. Noticing and highlighting coping skills makes people much more likely to use these resources.

Another aspect of the solution-oriented approach is to use skills and abilities the person or family has already developed in other areas and transfer them to help solve problems:

Milton Erickson once worked with a woman called "Ma" (Rossi, 1980), who had always wanted to learn to read and write, but had never been able to overcome her block to these goals. She was not given the chance to acquire these skills when young, and at age 16 she resolved that she would learn. At the age of 20, she hit upon the idea of taking in teachers as boarders and having them teach her to read and write. In the years that followed, her boarders and then her children relentlessly tried to teach her, all to no avail. She would become frightened and go blank whenever anyone tried to explain reading and writing to her.

At the age of 70, still unable to read, she came in contact with Erickson. He promised her that she would be reading and writing within three weeks and that he would ask her to do nothing that she did not already know how to do. She was skep-tical but intrigued. First, he asked her to pick up a pencil. He told her to pick it up any haphazard fashion, as a baby would. Next, he asked her to make some marks on a paper, any scrib-bling marks, as a baby unable to write might do. Then he asked her to draw some straight lines, as she would mark a board that she wanted to saw or lay out a garden when she wanted to plant a straight row. She could make the lines up and down or across or diagonally. Then she was to draw some donut holes and the two halves of a donut when it is broken in half. Finally, she was to draw the two sides of a gabled roof. He instructed her to continue practicing these marks even though she did not see their relevance.

At the next session, Erickson told her that the only difference between a pile of lumber and a house was that the latter was merely put together. She agreed, but again did not see the rele-vance. With Erickson's guidance, she put those marks together to make all the letters of the alphabet. When she had completed that, Erickson explained that she had just learned to write all the letters. Spelling words was merely a matter of putting letters together, he told her. After getting her to put the letters together, he told her that she now knew how to form words. Erickson got her to name certain words because each word has a name, just as each farm animal has a name. Gradually, he maneuvered her into writing a sentence and had her name all the words in it. The sentence read, "Get going Ma and put some grub on the table." When she said this aloud, she realized it was just like talking (her late husband had often used this phrase). The translation into reading was easily made within a three-week period.

People who have been abused have unrecognized strengths and resources that can be used in their healing.

A final aspect of solution-oriented therapy is that it typically focuses on the present and the future and is organized
around a clear definition of the presenting concern and a
good sense of where clients want to end up after treatment is
complete.

A while ago, Bill was given a stern talking to by
Steve de Shazer, developer of another solution-based approach, about the inadvisability of doing workshops on
treating people who have been sexually abused. "You're
focusing on the problem, not the solution! We never see
people who have been sexually abused at our clinic; we
only see people who have complaints and want to have
something happen for them." He's got a point, but we
thought the benefit of reaching people who would generally never come to a workshop or read a book on brief therapy or solution-based therapy outweighed the risks. In
addition, our approach acknowledges and includes the
problem and solution parts of the situation, not just the solution. All psychotherapy must be individualized, because
each person is unique. But there are recognizable patterns
in groups, and as long as one doesn't impose one's ideas on
clients, it is sometimes helpful to speak about general patterns and strategies.

On another note, Bill had been sexually abused by his
grandfather when he was younger (a one-time incident—
nothing as horrendous as some of the abuse stories he has
heard, but it had an impact nonetheless). So Bill had a special interest in the topic and some sense of what people
who have been abused have been through. Also, one of the
things that Bill's grandfather had done while perpetrating
the molestation was use confusion. Bill was left with a dis-
taste for confusion, leading to a habit (verging on a compulsion) of wanting to make things clear. You, the reader,

are the beneficiary of his compulsion to clarity. So, not everything that derives from sexual abuse is necessarily a patho-
logical hindrance, as some more pathology-based theorists
and writers imply.

Bill O'Hanlon
Bob Bertolino

January 1998

ACKNOWLEDGMENTS

*T*hank you to family, friends, and colleagues who made corrections and suggestions on the manuscript: Christine Bertolino, Pat Holterman-Hommes, Kevin Thompson, Nancy Newport, Steffanie O'Hanlon, Michael Martin, and Karen Sands.

Bob would like to thank the supportive staff at Youth in Need in St. Charles, Missouri, for providing rich clinical experiences and friendship. The faculty in the Department of Counseling and Family Therapy at St. Louis University also deserves mention for their words of wisdom and unwavering support. Thank you to all my clients, who have enriched my life and taught me. Thanks also to Kelly Franklin, senior editor at John Wiley & Sons, for her vision of this as being an important and necessary book. I would like to extend a special thank-you to Bill and Steffanie for their friendship, encouragement, humor, and deviance. And in particular, to Bill, for simply being who he is.

Bill would like to thank Steffanie for the valuing, inclusion, and love; Callie, Chris, Mara, Carla, Judy, and others for the on-the-job training; Mary Nathan, for the constant assistance, caring, and support; Angie Hexum for keeping me as her stepfather (and for occasionally retaining me as her father); my siblings Suzanne, Terry, Paul, and Dick for showing me such active support during a difficult few years; and my son Patrick, with the hope that time will heal us both.

CONTENTS

EVEN FROM
A BROKEN
WEB

CHAPTER ONE

A Break in the Web

A MAN WAS IMPRISONED for years. One day in the prison shop where he worked, his eyes caught little bits of bright wire amidst the shavings on the floor. He began gathering them and saving them in a bottle in his room to brighten things up a bit in the cell. After years of confinement, he was finally released from prison and brought the bottle full of wires with him to remind him of his years there. Now an old man and unable to work, he spent days waking at the exact hour the warden had decreed the prisoners should awaken and going to sleep at the usual prison lights out time. He paced back and forth in his rooms in the same patterns he had while confined to his cell, four steps forward and four steps back. After some time of this, he grew frustrated one day and smashed the bottle. He found the mass of rusted wires stuck together in the shape of a bottle. (Lord, 1990, p. 3)

In recent years, more and more people have been coming to therapy with the primary presenting problem of the after-effects of sexual abuse. Reports of sexual abuse were once considered fantasy phenomena, Oedipal or Electra impulses, or simply a secondary concern. Over the years, views began to shift and most clinicians now take reports of childhood sexual abuse more at face value.

Like many clinicians in the mid-1970s, Bill started hearing more reports of sexual abuse from his clients. As he learned more about how to work successfully with people who had experienced abuse, he became curious about what the sexual abuse and trauma experts (the folks who were writing books and teaching workshops) were saying and doing. What he found surprised him because most of the models and methods he discovered in the literature and workshops were very different from his approach. These models were mainly oriented to long-term treatment, but Bill's clients usually resolved their concerns in brief courses of therapy. Other approaches primarily focused on the past, and having clients regress and relive traumatic events as a way of healing. Bill's work was generally present and future oriented and rarely involved regression and reexperiencing of the trauma. Years after Bill began to shape his ideas, Bob discovered Bill's model and felt it complemented his approach for working with the aftereffects of sexual abuse and trauma. Ultimately, this evolved into a collaborative effort.

Our mission has been to develop and refine a respectful approach that taps into and honors the inherent healing abilities that people possess. Our discussion of basic trauma theory may be familiar territory for many readers because our understanding of what happens as a result of trauma is similar to traditional models. Where we offer something new is in the area of interventions. This involves a major departure in treatment philosophy: Our approach is less traumatic, less difficult, less painful, and less disruptive to people's lives. This book is about these ideas, and an alternative way of working with people suffering from the aftereffects of sexual abuse.

FROM BUDDHIST TO PERSONALITY:
A THEORY OF RESPONSE TO TRAUMA

Although we may have forgotten most of what we learned in graduate school about human development, one thing did stick with us. Piaget's work showed that all children are born Buddhists. What does this mean? Piaget showed that children do not really distinguish between themselves and the world (Gruber & Voneche, 1977). They have a Buddhist view of life in that they see themselves as one with everything. They have diffuse external boundaries and make no distinctions between self and other. For infants then, it is, "I am the same as you, and we are the same as the chair."

In this culture, as children grow, we teach them to be people with distinct and separate personalities. As this process proceeds, people develop a sense that they live in a body and that body is separate from other bodies. Their reality becomes, "I am Bob and this is Bill, and you are different from me, and we are both different from the chair." Thus, children develop a sense of identity and self boundaries. These personalities we create are located inside people, or as Gregory Bateson (1972) said, in "our bag of bones." Within these self boundaries, we have many facets of ourselves. For example, Bill and Bob both have musical parts. Bill also has a "ham" part that people see in workshops, a comedic part, and shy part. Bob has a competitive part that shows up in sports, a quiet part, and a sarcastic part. These are just a few aspects, but they give us a sense of who we are and each of us can say, "That's me."

We also have feeling parts and memories. Memories are not always available to the conscious mind. Have you ever looked at a picture—purportedly of you at a young age—and not recognized it? Although it is unfamiliar, the picture may have invoked a sense self-presence, expressed as the feeling, "I don't remember that, but I still have a sense that is me." In addition to the sense of self-presence, we also develop a sense of continuity or *narrative self:* "I came from my childhood and certain things affected me and now I'm here and I have a sense of my future. There are different parts of me, but they are all me." We may have various and occasionally contradictory feelings, thoughts, sensations, and experiences, but we consider them to be *ours* and create a relatively coherent sense of self (O'Hanlon, 1993, in press).

It is usually different when children have been sexually abused or intruded on in other ways. When children are intruded on before they develop a very good sense of themselves, they tend to become confused about boundaries. They lose sight of who they are, where their self ends, and where other people begin. This loss of self doesn't just result from physical or sexual intrusions but can also stem from experiential intrusion.

Experiential intrusion occurs when an experience attributed to a person contradicts that person's felt experience. In an abusive situation, the abuser might say to a child, "You like this," or "You feel good." Because the child is most likely not feeling good and, in fact, is scared or numb, the abuser's attribution of experience is a particular type of intrusion.

A story that Cloé Madanes often tells trainees illustrates the complexities of human communication (Simon, 1982/1992). She relates that as her then husband, Jay Haley, went to the door to drive their daughter Magali to school each morning, Madanes would tell the daughter to take a jacket. Magali would say that it was not cold outside, but her mother would insist it was. This debate occurred each morning as Haley patiently waited. After awhile, he would end the bantering by saying, "Your mother is cold today, you'd better take a jacket."

This example is the opposite of intrusion. He didn't intrude experientially and say, "You have to feel cold." He asked Magali to take a jacket, but did not ask her to experience something she wasn't experiencing. He didn't attempt to attribute experience to her. Bill found this technique to be helpful with his children at bedtime. He would say, "You go to bed, I'm tired!" which the children experienced very differently than the intrusive, "It's time to go to bed, you're tired and cranky."

Most children experience relatively benign intrusions on a regular basis. Some children, however, routinely experience more harmful intrusions.

When intrusion happens early enough and often enough, people can get confused about where their external boundaries are. When the intrusion is severe, children compensate for the lack of external boundaries by developing really solid *internal* boundaries (it seems that people need boundaries somewhere). Sometimes these internal boundaries become so impassable or strong that the person is unaware of one part or another. In extreme cases, this may lead to multiple personalities. Herman (1992) related, "Traumatic memories have a tendency to become disconnected from their source and to take on a life of their own" (p. 34). In the case of multiple personalities, aspects of self seem to have lives of their own, memories of their own, and personalities of their own. This early, severe, and consistent intrusion before the development of a coherent sense of a self lends itself to more distinct divisions within people. Thus, the outer boundaries remain diffuse, but the internal boundaries become rigid (see Figure 1.1).

AFTEREFFECTS IN 3-D: DISSOCIATED, DISOWNED, AND DEVALUED ASPECTS OF SELF

Most people generally have different facets of their personalities, as well as a sense of an integrated self. When people subjected to trauma split internally and develop rigid boundaries, the sense of integrated self is lost. Most people are not so split that they experience multiple selves, but more often they separate one or more aspects of their experience. We call this the 3-Ds of the aftereffects of sexual abuse: *Dissociation, Disowning,* and *Devaluing.* Aspects of experience that

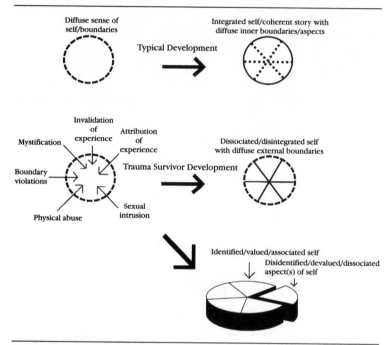

FIGURE 1.1   Dissociative/Devalued Aspects of Self in the After-effects of Trauma.

are dissociated, disowned, and devalued can be perceptions, thoughts, memories, sensations, or feelings (see Figure 1.2).

Dissociation refers to a person's sense of being split off from the self or some aspect of the self. Most people who have been abused or go through trauma dissociate (the word *most* serves as a reminder that not everyone has the same response to trauma). Because abuse and trauma can be so physically, painfully, and emotionally overwhelming, people split off from their experience. They separate experientially from their bodies or emotions. Dissociation is a perfectly normal and appropriate coping response to trauma (Dolan, 1991; Herman, 1992).

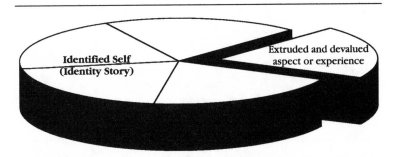

FIGURE 1.2 Dissociated/Disowned/Devalued Aspects of Self.

The second aspect of the trauma reaction is *disowning*. It is fairly typical for the experience of sexual abuse to be dissociated, but some facet of self also gets disowned: "It's not happening in my body or in my experience," (dissociation) and, "It's not me" (disowned). It is possible to simultaneously disown and dissociate: "I didn't get angry," or "I didn't get sexually abused," or "Those sexual parts of my body aren't me." Disowned facets of self are usually experienced and referred to as "it," as in "It just takes me over."

The third aspect that seems to be crucial to experiencing something as a problem or a symptom is *devaluing*. People who devalue aspects of themselves may feel or think things like, "I'm bad," "Anger is bad," "Sexuality is bad," "My body is bad," or "I'm bad if I feel or experience these things." The person attributes negativity to the experience that has been dissociated and disowned.

A typical component that people in the aftereffects of sexual abuse dissociate, disown, and devalue is sexual sensations. They may also apply the 3-Ds to bodily memories, anger, and sensory memories or sensations. The aspects of the self that are dissociated, disowned, or devalued often resurface as the symptoms that bring people to therapy.

INHIBITION AND INTRUSION: TWO
KINDS OF AFTEREFFECTS

The problems arising from the abuse are like a rheostat (dimmer switch) that controls the brightness of lights. For some people, it is as if their internal rheostat has been turned down. Experience is diminished or *inhibited.* Persons suffering from this aftereffect might describe a situation where they begin to have sex with their partner, whom they love, and they become numb and do not feel anything. Their sexual sensations are inhibited. People on the flip side feel as if the lights have been turned up so high they are blinding. People who experience the aftereffects of trauma in this way may feel compulsively sexual, go out and have sex with someone they do not know, and then feel very badly about it afterward. That is an *intrusive,* domineering, or compulsive experience. Either the intensity is turned down and the person does not experience it, or it is turned up so much that it feels overwhelming (see Table 1.1):

A client who was abused had a nickname when she was younger: "Sunshine." She had to be very happy and smile all the time. As an adult, whenever she would become angry at somebody (which was rare), she would smile when telling the person she was angry. So others never got the sense that she was really angry. Then, every once in a while somebody would say something and she would go into an absolute rage. She and the unwitting antagonist would be shocked: it was so unlike her.

Anger was both missing (diminished) and intrusive in her life. First, it was diminished, "I'm the kind of person who doesn't show anger." Then it intruded on her, "It seemed like it wasn't me." A certain aspect of experience (perception,

TABLE 1.1
INHIBITION AND INTRUSION:
POLARITIES OF TROUBLESOME AFTEREFFECTS OF TRAUMA

Inhibited/Lacking	Intrusive/Compulsive
No sexual response/ sensations	Compulsive/"addictive" sexuality
No anger	Rage
No memories (might be lacking only visual, auditory, gustatory, olfactory, or kinesthetic, or some combination)	Flashbacks (might be visual, auditory, gustatory, olfactory, or kinesthetic, or some combination)
No body awareness; lack of connection with certain body parts (e.g., the arms)	Somatic/medical symptoms; eating disorders; self-mutilation

feeling, sensation, memory, or automatic thought) feels very dissociated and automatic for that person. Either that aspect goes missing from the person's life (becomes inhibited or diminished) or it intrudes. The use of the word "it" is deliberate since this aspect of experience feels like an "it" rather than a part of the person. These aftereffects are not general (like "issues of control"), but specific (like visual memories), which is why the therapy we do can be brief (but we'll get into that later).

THE MISSING ROOMMATE: INHIBITION, INTRUSION, AND DISIDENTIFICATION

The analogy of the missing roommate nicely illustrates these dynamics. Imagine there are a bunch of people who live in a house and they all decide to get rid of a roommate because he's bad and not like them. So they lock him out and change the locks. He comes to the door trying to get back in and pounds on it for a while. He wants to get back in, so he is persistent, but the roommates tell each other to ignore him, thinking he will go away. After a while, he becomes exhausted and slumps against the door. They think that he's gone away and will not cause any more trouble. For quite a while, it seems to have worked. But he's really just sleeping outside the door. Eventually, something wakes him up, and he decides that he really has to get back in the house. He pounds on the door again but gets no response and becomes tired again. Finally, he becomes really desperate and crashes in through the front window.

That's what flashbacks, body memories, sensory sensations, or self-harming behavior are like. All of a sudden, the aspect that went missing wakes up and says, "I want back in! I am part of you! I want back in and I'm going to get attention!" When an aspect goes missing and is dissociated, devalued, and disowned, it develops a mind or life of its own. It's disidentified and sort of drifts off on its own, typically in a way that is destructive in relationship to oneself. It doesn't have many checks and balances because it's not in relationship with oneself. First, it is missing (inhibited), and then it is all too present (intrusive).

THE UNEXPERIENCED EXPERIENCE MODEL

The traditional model of working with clients who have been abused could be called the *unexperienced experience model.* The idea is that people who go through a trauma such as sexual abuse dissociate during that time as a way to cope. They dissociate from their emotions, sensory sensations, or perceptions, or other experiences. And the traditional model holds that since they dissociate, they never really experienced the trauma. This lack of connection with the traumatic experience leads to the development of symptoms in the present. Therefore, the problem lies in the past, and to resolve it, the therapist must help these clients regress back to the traumatic time so they can remember, reexperience, and relive what was previously dissociated.

According to this traditional model, during the reexperiencing and reliving of the trauma, the person needs to feel the original emotions that were not previously experienced. This process entails a lot of catharsis, abreaction, and expression of emotion. This sort of treatment—working through—is a torturous endeavor. A common assumption is, "For you to properly heal, it will become worse before it gets better." Under this approach to therapy, people have to go through traumatic experiences over and over again and replay their memory loops no matter how painful they may be. Because of the pain involved, it is not unusual for people to avoid or drop out of therapy, or to say things such as, "This hurts too much," "I can't do this," or "This is too hard."

Traditional therapy focused on reliving the experience is also a long and arduous process. Because the trauma is deeply seated within the person, the healing process necessitates a connection with the core issues. If the treatment is not long-term, the person is seen as in denial or minimizing the situation, or the therapist or therapy itself is not addressing the necessary core issues.

Many clients become a lot more self-destructive during this difficult process. There is often an initiation of or an increase in self-mutilating or other self-harming behaviors such as suicide attempts or eating disorders. Typically, people's personal relationships will suffer greatly when being treated from this perspective. Often they don't want to be intimate or have sex with their partners, which can lead to blaming or further problems. This can be compounded if a partner disagrees with the treatment or feels it is making things worse.

The unexperienced experience model is based on the premise that for healing to occur, therapy must be long-term, regressive, and cathartic, and involve intensive memory work. This means that these clients can expect to reexperience the trauma and pain in and out of therapy for years *while they are getting better*. In this approach, a person's stuckness is due to a lack of experience with the trauma, and the way to resolve it is through confrontation of the unconfronted, and acceptance of the unaccepted. The unexperienced experience model is an interesting concept, but it is not based on any scientific truths. We have a different idea. Our belief is not that clients need to reexperience their abuse, but rather, that they are experiencing it *over and over again*. They keep reliving the same experience, behaviors, thinking, emotions, and sensory responses again and again. Essentially, people have become locked into their experiences, or *frozen in time*. It is not that they live this every second of their lives; instead a piece of them, an aspect or experience, is frozen and keeps repeating, like a tape loop, some aspect of the abuse over and over again.

IN THE SHAPE OF A BOTTLE: PATTERNS OF VIEWING AND DOING

People frozen in their experiences characteristically develop particular, repetitive patterns of thinking and doing. These can shape the way these people perceive themselves and ultimately, how they show up in the world. They become molded in the form of their experience, like the prisoner described at the beginning of the chapter.

People become patterned in what we call the *viewing* and *doing* of the problem (O'Hanlon & Beadle, 1994; O'Hanlon & Weiner-Davis, 1989). There are recognizable, repetitive patterns in how they think about, make sense of, or put together their problem, and how they do their lives in the world:

❖ The *viewing* involves those patterns of thinking or attention that are harmful or ineffective for the person.

❖ The *doing* relates to actions or interactions that are harmful or ineffective for the person.

In later chapters, we'll discuss ways to help people change their patterns of doing and viewing. For now, we just want to point out that in people frozen in time, these past patterns repeat again and again in the present.

SYMPTOMATIC TRANCE AND HEALING TRANCE

Another way to think of the frozen-in-time idea is by thinking of it as a *symptomatic trance.*

In the late 1970s, Bill specialized in treating bulimia. He was struck by how many clients would come in and talk about their bulimic episodes as if they had been in trance. They would say, "I had the best of intentions. I was working on what we were talking about and all of a sudden I found myself coming out of a binge." It was as if they were waking up and someone else ("it") had done the binge. It was if these clients came back after the episode and then criticized themselves for bingeing. They would devalue themselves for bingeing and doing the compulsive behavior.

These descriptions sounded a lot like trance—with one exception. The bulimic trances were negative. Our experience with therapeutic trancework was that most of the time people would say, "I didn't want to come out, that was great! I was feeling valued, and the possibilities were endless." That was a *healing trance.* What the bulimics were describing in their experiences was also trancelike, only negative. We refer to this as *symptomatic trance* (Gilligan, 1987; O'Hanlon, 1993, in press; O'Hanlon & Martin, 1992).

This idea of symptomatic trance is very much like what is taught in family therapy. Family interaction can sometimes bring about symptomatic experience with people, especially when family members invalidate one another. One person is chosen as the scapegoat and gets invalidated. That person is the "bad one" who never does anything right, or who is labeled as a troublemaker in some way. Those inductions are very much like hypnotic inductions except they are negative in content.

R. D. Laing (1967) years ago wrote about social processes in families and society that essentially invite people to craziness. Some typical social inductions to problems include mystification, binds and double binds, violations of cross-generational or experiential boundaries in families, coalitions, secrets, predictions of failure or trouble, mind reading, and rigid role assignments. The same sort of processes can induce negative social trance inductions. Conversely, healing inductions involve validation, permission, respect for boundaries, possibility words, helpful distinctions, posthypnotic suggestions, and presuppositions of health and healing.

Perhaps the best articulation of this is by Michele Ritterman (1983) who has worked with political refugees who were tortured and repressed. She studied the social processes of symptom induction: how systematic attempts at brainwashing and devaluing of certain groups in a culture create symptomatic experiences. In addition to cultures, she also studied the induction of problems in smaller social groups including families. Finally, Ritterman looked at self-induction, also referred to as *negative self-hypnosis* (Araoz, 1985), which occurs when a person incorporates a symptom induction within the self. Ritterman found that the processes could be reversed or challenged by bringing people out of those negative, symptomatic inductions by doing individual, family, and social therapies (the latter of which included group therapy and social action initiatives).

People are in a negative, symptomatic trance when they are in their posttraumatic experience. Sometimes, just as in hypnosis, a person can develop a hypnotic cue, and go into a bad trance. They may smell or feel something that triggers them into their symptom trances. What people do with traumatic experiences often resembles what happens in healing trance. In therapeutic hypnosis, we learn about trance phenomena that people do automatically such as amnesia, analgesia, negative and positive hallucination, sensory distortions, and age regression or progression. These are similar to symptom phenomena that people present with when they come for the aftereffects of sexual abuse. With a hypnotic process, they can change their sensory experience. This seems to be the case with sexual abuse as people shift their sensory perceptual experience and bodily experience to recreate that original situation. Thus, when they are invited into a negative trance with a personal cue, they keep repeating the trauma again and again. They then experience invalidation, devaluing, and no sense of choice.

An interesting representation of this occurs in the movie *Dr. Strangelove or: How I Learned to Stop Worrying and Love the Bomb.* Dr. Strangelove, played by Peter Sellers, is a cold-war scientist who talks about winning a nuclear war and pushing the button to drop the bomb. Throughout the movie, he battles with his gloved hand (the one that would presumably push the button), which keeps rising up and reaching for his throat. His hand seems to move as if it has a mind of its own. This involuntary, automatic action is destructive and intrudes on him time after time. Dr. Strangelove's self-destructive hand is akin to the intrusiveness of traumatic experiences that have been dissociated, disowned, and devalued. The person's experience seems to turn on him or her in a most destructive and intrusive manner.

What is the difference between these symptomatic trances and healing trances? In our view, the main difference is valuing and a sense of choice. In the best healing trances, as mentioned, people typically experience a sense of choice and validation. Their hands may be lifting, like Dr. Strangelove's, but they like the experience. Both have a sense of being automatic, but one feels bad and coerced (symptomatic trance) and the other (healing trance) feels validating and freeing. This concept is summarized in Table 1.2.

WHEN YOU FEEL LIKE A NAIL, EVERYTHING SEEMS LIKE A
HAMMER: THE PAST BECOMES THE FUTURE

Another way in which people become frozen in time is by projecting the traumatic past or the troubled present into the future. This can lead to a life of further suffering and traumatization. Many therapists have treated clients who were abused as children, and then became involved in abusive relationships as adults.

TABLE 1.2 SYMPTOMATIC TRANCE → HEALING TRANCE	
Symptom Induction	**Healing Induction**
Invalidation; blame; violating boundaries	Validation; permission; respecting boundaries
Mystification; binds; double binds	Possibility words and phrases
Coalitions; secrets; negative dissociation	Helpful distinctions
Predictions of failure or trouble; threats	Posthypnotic suggestions; presuppositions of health/healing
Rigid role assignment; mind reading	Positive attributions; avoidance of intrusive interpretations
Repetition of negative experiences/injurious/self-injurious behavior	Opening of possibilities for changes in experience or behavior
Negative injunctions (You can't, you shouldn't, you will, you are)	Empowering/permissive affirmations (You can, it's okay, you may, you could, you have the ability to, you don't have to)
Repression; amnesia	Reversible forgetting/remembering

Symptomatic trance is repetitive and self-devaluing, and closes down possibilities. It is a repetition of past states of being that are not updated to fit with current contexts. Self as more than symptom is forgotten.

Healing trance is validating, empowering, and opens up possibilities. It is responsive to current contexts. Self as more than symptom is remembered.

When people begin to anticipate that their future will repeat the past or the present, they interact with others in different ways and they don't take actions that might create a better and different future. This creates a self-fulfilling prophecy. People feel condemned to a future that is determined by their past. They feel spoiled or damaged, and their lives begin more and more to reflect that view.

In the following chapters, we discuss ways of changing these symptomatic trances into healing trances, or of waking the person from trance altogether.

THE AFTEREFFECTS OF SEXUAL ABUSE: A CHANGING PHILOSOPHY

One of Bill's mentors was the late John Weakland of the Mental Research Institute Brief Therapy Project (personal communication, 1985). Several years ago during a visit to Palo Alto, California, the two had a discussion about the history of psychotherapy. Weakland said, "During the first 100 years, we were pretty arrogant. We thought we could make people's lives problem-free if we just did good enough and long enough therapy. But I think we have realized that we cannot do this. Why? Because life is just one damn thing after another, as the old saying goes. As a therapist, you are never going to make life problem-free because there are always going to be challenges along the road in life. You go through one developmental phase after another and new challenges appear. But the problem for people who come to therapy is that life has stopped being one damn thing after another and has become the same damn thing over and over. They experience, think, feel, interact in, and their bodies do, the same damn thing over and over again."

After thinking about that for a while, Bill realized that, as therapists, our job is to help people shift from doing the same damn thing over and over again back to doing one damn thing after another—and then the therapist should get out of their lives. That stuckness is what we are working with, that repetition of the old experience. We don't need to be in their lives forever to try and make everything better. We just want to help them with this frozen-in-timeness, and invite them to move on.

One way to do this is by the traditional model. We can get people to value what they have disowned by remembering and reliving it while we hold them in a long-term caring relationship in therapy. But there is another way of getting people moving that is much more present and future-oriented, doesn't usually take so long, and is not so painful or dangerous.

A BRIEF, RESPECTFUL APPROACH

We believe there is an alternative way to work with the aftereffects of sexual abuse that is far less intrusive than the traditional unexperienced experience model. We offer a respectful, clear model that emphasizes the strengths, abilities, and resources of clients. This approach, brief as it is, doesn't minimize or invalidate people's experiences. It calls for the acknowledgment, valuing, and validation of every facet of the client. It is a perspective in which clients are invited into collaborative conversations. In these conversations, we seek to help people see the possibilities, be accountable for what they do, and take actions that will help move them on into the kind of future they hope for.

This philosophy contributes to a therapy that is generally briefer, and a lot less torturous to go through than the traditional model. Although some people take longer than others to heal, our experience is that most can do it rapidly and in a less painful manner. Our orientation is toward helping clients to move on in a safe, respectful way. In fact, our clients teach us how they heal, and inform us as to what they need from therapy. This approach promotes each person's own unique sense of healing in determining the course of therapy.

We don't assume that clients need to go back and work through traumatic experiences and reclaim their feelings. Nor do we experientially intrude on people with our ideas and tell them that we know what they need do to heal ("You must remember or you are denying"). Instead, we orient them toward the present and future (while recognizing that if a client feels the need to go back and reexperience trauma, that is also acceptable). These clients have already suffered greatly. We want to help them to resolve their symptoms and reach their goals with as little additional suffering as possible.

This model involves working in the present toward the future through three general strategies:

1. Initially, we focus on the presenting concern, complaint, or symptom to help clients value, own, and associate to discarded aspects of themselves. This is *Moving on Method 1*.

2. Next, we help clients find workable alternatives to the currently unworkable patterns of doing and viewing of the problem that brought them to therapy. This is *Moving on Method 2*.

3. Finally, we help clients develop a clear sense of a future with possibilities. This is *Moving on Method 3*.

HOW TO MAKE THERAPY MORE
BRIEF AND GOAL-ORIENTED

How do you know if the person is experiencing the after-effects of sexual abuse and is stuck in that experience? Since it's not always a clear thing, and we don't want to intrude in and impose our beliefs on people's experiences ("You must remember your abuse to heal or explore repressed feelings," clients are sometimes told in the traditional model), we consider the complaint or problem as the best place to start. Thus, when someone complains about something, when something is bothering them, therapy begins.

In the beginning of therapy, we want to find out two things. First, what is the client complaining about? We need to stop and ascertain why the person is in therapy because this will give us a hint as to what we need to focus on resolving. Second, we want to find out how the person will know when the therapy is done. From these two pieces of information, we can gain a sense of where this client wants to go and what it may look like when the person gets there.

If clients come to therapy and say that they were sexually abused, we still want to know what the complaint is. Many people have been sexually abused and have gone to therapy for reasons other than their abuse. So we do not automatically orient to the sexual abuse and say, "You need to go back to your childhood and feel the feelings that you never felt." That's the therapist imposing on the client and intruding, saying, "I know what you need to do. Go there." We do not assume that the entire experience of sexual abuse is the problem. We want to hear about what it is that clients came in for, and where they want to go. There are clients who just want to know whether what they are experiencing is normal or valid or just want to have someone to tell about their abuse.

They may have problems that are unrelated to the sexual abuse.

Sometimes people will have a sense that they were abused, but are not sure. They might say something like, "When I go to have sex with my partner I go numb. I don't remember being abused, but I've been reading about it and this is one of the aftereffects." This is how we typically dialogue with these clients:

CLIENT: I think I was abused. I don't know. I just go numb.

THERAPIST: Going numb can be the result of many things. What gives you the sense that you were sexually abused?

CLIENT: I'm not sure. I just know that numbness during sex could mean that I was abused.

THERAPIST: Right. You're just not sure at this point, but it could mean a number of things. But what *is* clear to you is that you want to experience sex without numbness?

CLIENT: Yeah. Can you hypnotize me so I can remember if I was abused or not?

THERAPIST: I'm not sure that's going to be necessary or if it's a good idea. My sense is that you'd like to be able to experience sexuality with the partner you love, and if that involves remembering abuse, you are willing to do that. But if there are other ways to get to that experience, you'd be willing to try those ways, too, as long as you can be okay feeling the sexual feelings with your partner. Is that right?

CLIENT: Yes, that's what I want.

We suggest that we start with working on the sexuality. If there are unaccounted for memories, explorations of sexuality can help bring them to light. If there are not, this approach to therapy will not pressure the person to produce these memories. In this way, the therapy is client-driven, complaint-driven, and goal-oriented. It begins with the person's complaint, and is not theory or therapist determined. To us, this feels much more respectful of the client.

So what are the specific complaints people bring into therapy when they have been sexually abused? Many people who are suffering from the aftereffects of sexual abuse enter therapy when they feel inhibited or intruded on and have symptoms. When asked about their symptoms, people will usually say something like, "I have flashbacks." Then, if you ask in detail, they describe specific pictures, images, or memories. They may also describe it in other ways such as, "Occasionally my body feels as if I'm being raped," or "I can taste this terrible taste in my mouth, and it tastes like semen." They have specific kinds of flashbacks and intrusive memories, or specific kinds of lack of memories or lack of experience. That's where we start, not with some vague notion of "working through their childhood sexual abuse." We want to help them either start to experience or stop experiencing something, based on their concerns or complaints.

In the next three chapters, we describe three methods for helping people move on from the aftereffects of sexual abuse trauma. This approach differs from traditional treatment models in that it is present- to future-oriented and collaborative. In addition, although this approach acknowledges the damage clients have suffered, it calls for the recognition and utilization of the strengths they possess.

Summary Points
Chapter One

❖ People who have been traumatized often split off facets of themselves and their experience.

❖ The aftereffects of trauma can be characterized as a 3-D model: People dissociate, disown, and devalue aspects of themselves.

❖ Presenting symptoms can be the result of this 3-D process in that the missing components of a person's experience begin to be experienced in a diminished, inhibited way (like few memories of childhood or numbness during sex) or in an intrusive, dominating way (like intrusive, disturbing flashbacks or obsessive sexual fantasies).

❖ People experience their symptoms as if they are in a trance, having a sense that things are occurring automatically and that some facets of themselves or their experiences are bad, but feeling powerless to do anything about those "bad" parts or experiences.

❖ Traditional therapeutic approaches treat the dissociated, disowned, or devalued aspects by encouraging the person to reexperience the original trauma. This takes quite a long time and often results in a loss of functioning and an increase in self-destructiveness of the person.

❖ This model presents three alternative directions for treatment that are not focused on the past, but are present- and future-oriented:

Moving on Method 1—Revalue and include devalued and disowned experience or aspects of self.

Moving on Method 2—Change repetitive, unworkable patterns.

Moving on Method 3—Orient the person to a future in which things can be different and the past will not be endlessly repeated.

CHAPTER
TWO

Even from a
Broken Web

Permission, Validation,
and Inclusion

A WOMAN WHO HAD been ritually abused came to Bill for therapy. During one of her sessions, a part emerged and spoke to him. It was a devil named Astaroth. He mostly growled, was enraged, and threatening. Astaroth began threatening to kill the client and do terrible things to Bill's genitals. Then he left about as quickly as he had come. When the woman returned, she was very upset. It seemed to her that Astaroth was a devil that was possessing her. She wondered if perhaps we might consider an exorcism.

For a brief moment, Bill seriously considered an exorcism. Quickly, he reconsidered. He remembered that Astaroth was ultimately the woman, albeit in a different and distorted form. Doing an exorcism would be like saying this part of the client is no good and she has to get rid of it. She was already doing that.

So Bill started having conversations with Astaroth. He actually had a pretty good sense of humor, for a devil. He laughed at some of Bill's jokes. For example, at one point Astaroth told Bill that it was his job to kill the woman. Bill asked him if it was a good job, that is, did he get any benefits or a good retirement plan with the job? He burst out laughing despite himself.

Bill also asked him about this plan to kill her. What was the purpose? He told Bill he must kill her to protect her. Bill was a bit confused by this logic, but persisted, gently asking questions until Astaroth told Bill that he had to kill her to ensure that no one else would abuse her. Bill mentioned that he had heard a quotation recently, "There's nothing as dangerous as an idea, when it's the only one you have." Astaroth seemed quiet and thoughtful after that. At the beginning of the next *meeting, Astaroth was present as the woman walked in the door. He told Bill that she had a razor in her purse and had plans to hurt herself. He asked Bill to take the razor and throw it away. So after a while, Astaroth and Bill developed a good relationship. During the course of the next few weeks, Astaroth turned into a little girl, who had been abused. Then, the little girl turned into the woman.*

As Carl Jung said, "Every part of us that we do not love will regress and become more primitive." We are suggesting that the things that people bring as symptoms or problems to therapy are hints about the parts of themselves that they haven't loved and that have regressed and become more primitive.

In Chapter 1, we noted that people who are intruded on physically or experientially dissociate, disown, and devalue aspects of themselves. This has paradoxical results. On the one hand, these people are intruded on by painful memories, sensations, and perceptions, that crash into them like the missing roommate described earlier. On the other hand, pleasant and wanted memories, sensations, and perceptions from past, present, or future are inhibited or absent as well. Judith Lewis Herman (1992) wrote:

> In the aftermath of an experience of overwhelming danger, the two contradictory responses of intrusion and constriction establish an oscillating rhythm. This dialectic of opposing psychological states is perhaps the most characteristic feature of the post-traumatic syndromes. Since neither the intrusive nor the numbing symptoms allow for the integration of the traumatic event, the alteration between these two extreme states might be understood as an attempt to find a satisfactory balance between the two. But balance is precisely what the traumatized person lacks.

She finds herself caught between the extremes of amnesia or of reliving the trauma, between floods of intense, overwhelming feelings and arid states of no feeling at all, between irritable, impulsive action and complete inhibition of action. (p. 47)

The dichotomy between overwhelming feelings and no feelings creates an untenable bind as the person attempts to negotiate aspects of the self or experience that are at war with each other. In describing a traumatized combat veteran, Kardiner and Spiegel (1947) relate:

He had, in fact, a profound reaction to violence of any kind and could not see others being injured, hurt or threatened. . . . [However] he claimed that he felt like suddenly striking people and that he had become very pugnacious toward his family. (p. 128)

This man illustrates the paradox to which we were referring. He was both repelled by and compelled to violence. Survivors of sexual abuse seem to be in a similar position as they too, deal with the intersection of opposing experiences: inhibition and intrusion. It is like traffic gridlock.

Herman (1992) deemed the idea of opposing psychological states to be the *Dialectic of Trauma*. She speculates that contradictory responses of intrusion and constriction establish a sequential repetition in a search for balance. However, balance or inclusion is what the abuse survivor lacks. It is as if the person is trying to fit both of these parts through a doorway saying, "After you, Alphonse. No, after you, Gaston. No, after you, Alphonse . . ." Then both try to get through the door but there doesn't seem to be enough room. There is a way for both to get through the door. It comes from research on hypnosis, and we call it the "Inclusive Self."

TRANCE LOGIC AND THE INCLUSIVE SELF
OR HOW YOU CAN BE TWO PLACES AT ONCE

So what do we do with these seemingly oppositional polarities, or how can a person be two places at once? Years ago, Martin Orne (1959) and colleagues did some experiments on the phenomenon of "trance logic." In their experiments, deeply hypnotized subjects were trained to negatively hallucinate (not see) a chair. While hypnotized, the subjects were put in a room with a chair that they could not see due to the trance phenomena. They were then given a task that would involve them walking toward and bumping into the chair. However, each time the directive was given, the subjects avoided the chair that was in their path. When questioned about this, the subjects reported that they avoided the chair, but did not see it. It appeared as if they were both seeing and not seeing the chair simultaneously. What Orne and his associates discovered was that people in trance had the ability to hold two contradictory perceptions at the same time. This they deemed to be trance logic.

This kind of logic, which appears to be available to people at a different level of self from their normal processing, can hold seemingly contradictory ideas, perceptions, and feelings in a way that allows both to exist and be valid. As F. Scott Fitzgerald once said, "The test of a first-rate intelligence is the ability to hold two opposed ideas in the mind at the same time and still retain the ability to function."

For survivors, the Inclusive Self represents a place where they can both remember and not remember their abuse. One client said, "My mind didn't remember, but the cells of my body did." At the level of the Inclusive Self, the person can both feel sexual and, at the same time, not feel sexual. As the poet Adrienne Rich said: "Anger and tenderness—my selves. And now I can believe they breathe in me as angels and not as polarities. Anger and tenderness—the spider's genius. To spin and weave in one moment anywhere. Even from a broken web" (quoted in Whyte, 1989). The therapist's task is to help people to "spin and weave" at once—to develop and connect with their Inclusive Self:

A client reported that she never really experienced everyday life. She always saw it as if it were being displayed on a movie screen before her. Her inner experience was dominated by memories of the sexual abuse she had suffered in childhood. She was invited to close her eyes and focus inside, and it was suggested that she could allow both the memories and everyday life to be included in her experience. She could remember and not remember at the same time. After she opened her eyes, she reported that she had instantly begun to see everyday life on one side of a split screen and the abuse memories on the other side of the screen. When she emerged from trance, she said that for the first time in her awareness, the abuse memories were not dominating her experience.

The Inclusive Self, then, is the whole person. It is the "bigger self" that contains and transcends the polarities. Figure 2.1 shows the aspects of the Inclusive Self. The aspects of ourselves that we identify with and think of as ourselves make up the Identified Self (the Identity Story). These are the facets of our experience that we recognize as ourselves. For example, Roger may think of himself as a "nice guy" and identify with things he does that fit that self-image or story. If he happens to do something mean or selfish, he may disregard that or think of it as bad (the devalued, disidentified aspect of self). But there may be times when he is both nice and selfish. Embracing both components is the job of the Inclusive Self. The Identified Self also includes what our friend Stephen Gilligan calls "Alien Voices" (Gilligan, personal

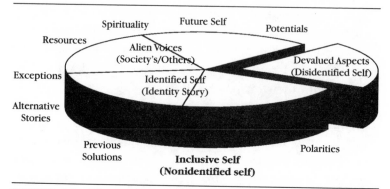

FIGURE 2.1   The Inclusive Self: An Antidote to Devalued, Dissociated and Disowned Aspects of Self. The Therapist Acknowledges All Aspects of the Client's Experience and Invites the Client into a Valuing Relationship and Possibility Available with Himself or Herself and Life.

communication, 1991). These are the influences of society and other people, usually our intimates, that we have incorporated into our view of ourselves. For example, a man may decide that he is not the kind of person who cries or wears dresses because he has incorporated the influences of others into his definition of what males are. After so many years of living with these voices and influences, we have come to experience them as part of ourselves.

In addition, the Inclusive Self is where other aspects of the self reside including the disidentified aspects of the self (that are experienced, but seen as not part of one's identity and as unacceptable). We have already discussed this when describing the 3-D model in Chapter 1. Outside the experiential self, there are nonarticulated, nonidentified facets of experience. Foremost among these facets are the exceptions to the usual patterns of how the person acts and views him- or herself. The solution-oriented approach (de Shazer, 1988;

Dolan, 1991; O'Hanlon & Weiner-Davis, 1988) is predicated on the idea that people have solutions to their problems but haven't noticed them. By asking about and orienting the person's attention to exceptions (times when the problem hasn't been as bad or has not happened when it was expected), the therapist and client can identify some aspects of self that were previously not obvious. By asking the client to deliberately use behaviors and viewpoints from those exceptions in the future, often the person changes his or her self-view, or what the person identifies as the self (Identity Story):

A young man was referred to therapy complaining that since he had been raped by a male counselor he had seen when he was a teenager some 10 years before, he had been having compelling fantasies about sexually abusing children. He was suicidal and homicidal when he arrived in therapy, in part because he loathed himself for having such horrible fantasies, and in part because he felt that he was about to act on those fantasies. If he did act on the fantasies, he would have to kill the child he had abused (to save the child from the kind of torturous life he had led) and then kill himself (because he could not live with himself if he acted out his fantasies). In the ensuing discussion, he recounted that his life was no longer worth living because he had wanted to serve children in some capacity (first as a schoolteacher, then as a stay-at-home father) and now that he had become unsafe for children, those paths were no longer open to him. As more information emerged, though, it became clear to both client and therapist that this man had protected children for the previous 10 years. His story about himself began to change as the therapist began to explore how the client had restrained himself from acting on his fantasies for so long. He

*began to feel himself to be much more in control than he had
felt when he first arrived in the therapist's office.*

Some aspects of the Inclusive Self might be thought of as
beyond the personal (transpersonal) as well, but clients and
therapists might be more comfortable thinking of them as
deep human potentials. For some, this involves getting in
touch with and articulating a connection with God, spiritu-
ality, or a higher self. For others, it means connecting with
their soul:

*A woman in therapy was berating herself for getting angry.
She felt she was ugly and unacceptable when she got angry
and had no right to feel that way. When asked if she could
imagine anyone who loved her that would be able to accept
her when she was feeling angry, she initially could not think
of anyone. Soon, her face softened as she quietly reported that
Jesus would accept her no matter what she was feeling. It was
suggested that she invite Jesus to be with her when she felt
angry. The next time she got angry, she imagined Jesus
putting a hand on her shoulder and smiling at her. This
helped the process of including anger into her self-identity.*

Lastly, the Inclusive Self contains a sense of the future self
that will develop. This idea of who a person will be in the future influences how one sees the self in the present. Chapter
Four explores this aspect of the Inclusive Self in more detail.

MAKING FRIENDS WITH YOUR DEMONS:
PERMISSION, INCLUSION, AND VALIDATION

One way to think of the presenting concern is that it reflects
an injunction. There are two kinds of injunctions:

1. *Inhibiting Injunctions.* (Have to/Should/Must, as in, "You must always be perfect," or "I have to hurt myself," or "I should always smile and be happy."

2. *Intrusive/Compulsive Injunctions.* Can't/Shouldn't/Don't, as in, "You shouldn't feel sexual feelings," or "I can't be angry."

These injunctions are conclusions that the person has made about him- or herself or ideas that other people have suggested or told the person are true. Tapping into the Inclusive Self allows the person to undo the inhibiting or intrusive effects of these injunctions.

We have found three useful methods for helping clients process their experience at the level of the Inclusive Self:

1. *Give permission* for experience.

2. *Include* seemingly opposite or contradictory aspects of experience.

3. *Validate and value* whatever experience the person is having at the moment.

Giving Permission

Our task as therapists is to give the freeing permission that would undo the limiting, devaluing injunction. Just as there are two kinds of injunctions, there are also two kinds of permission:

1. *Permission to.* "You can."

2. *Permission not to have to.* "You don't have to."

Although you can give either permission, we have found it more useful to give both permissions at the same time.

For example, "You can feel angry, and you don't have to feel angry." Or, "It's okay to be sexual, and you don't have to be sexual." If you only give one type of permission, the person may feel pressured to experience only one part of the equation or may find the other side emerging in a more compelling and disturbing way. For example, if you say, "It's okay to remember," the client might respond, "But I don't want to remember!" If you say instead, "It's okay to remember, and you don't have to remember," your client won't typically experience a bounce-back response.

Remember that you are giving permission for *experience,* not an action. Be careful when giving permission about actions. One could say, "It's okay to feel like cutting yourself, and you don't have to feel like cutting yourself," but it wouldn't be a good idea to say, "It's okay to cut yourself, and you don't have to cut yourself." Never give permission for harmful, destructive behavior.

Binds

Sometimes the person is stuck with dueling or seemingly opposite injunctions operating simultaneously. For example, "You must be perfect" is paired with "You never do anything right!" Or "You have to remember your abuse, and you can't remember the abuse."

Inclusion

A way to undo these binds is to suggest the possibility of having seeming opposites or contradictions coexist without conflict. For example, "You can remember and not remember the abuse." Or "You can feel sexual and not feel sexual at the same time." Or "You can be angry and calm all in one moment." How does this work in practice:

Bill had a new client named Josie. Josie came into a session very agitated and told him that she had something she had to tell him, but was terrified to talk about. Bill told her it was okay not to tell him until she was comfortable enough to do so. Josie responded by saying that she had *to tell him. Bill told her to go ahead and tell him right away then. She said, "But I can't tell you. I'm too afraid." Bill finally understood Josie's dilemma and said, "Okay, I know this may not make sense, but what I want to say can be understood somewhere deeply inside. You can tell me and not tell me at the same time." In response to this, Josie closed her eyes and her hands began to move in a very automatic way. They were doing some sort of elaborate movement that reminded Bill of hand dancing he had seen done by Thai performers. After some time, she opened her eyes and smiled, obviously relieved. "There," she said, "you were right. I told you and didn't tell you at the same time. My hands told you the whole story of my abuse. Now I can tell you in words." "That's good," Bill thought to himself, "because I didn't get the hand thing." Josie went on to tell Bill what had happened to her and how she was threatened that if she told anyone she and the person she told would be killed. Thus the terror. Telling was a great relief, once the bind was broken by including both sides of the dialectic.*

Allowing both sides of the dialectic brings to mind the question: What's the difference between therapy that goes in one ear and out the other and therapy that really moves people? The distinction that we make is therapy that makes a difference must somehow get down into the person's experience. The Inclusive Self methods we have detailed seem to accomplish this by bypassing the person's cognitive perception of the problem. It forgoes Aristotelian logic where things are understood as "either/or" and allows the person to process at a different level. When given the opportunity and permission to process on this level, survivors can find ways of resolving seeming contradictions in their experience.

Validation and Valuing

People who have been abused sometimes have the sense that their experience is "wrong" or invalid in some way. We respond to this by valuing and validating all that they are experiencing in the current moment, especially whatever they have been experiencing as unacceptable, bad, or wrong:

Bill saw a man, Mark, who had a severe case of obsessive compulsive disorder. Mark told Bill about the many intrusive obsessions he had. Mark's job was related to communication and teaching about communication. He became so obsessed with thinking about how human beings communicate that he couldn't put words and meanings together. Mark also suffered from another obsession. When he was talking to someone, he would have this very vivid image of their rectum right in front of his face. As you might imagine, this was just a little intrusive to his conversations. He would also develop this tension in his jaw and his neck and become terrified that he would have what he called "the Big Stutter." The Big Stutter was Mark's name for his fear that he would just freeze up and not be able to communicate at all. This was his idea of hell, since he lived to communicate. Mark had many other obsessions, which we won't detail here. If one went away, another would immediately take its place. He was essentially symptomatic from the moment he woke up until the moment he went to sleep.

Mark didn't believe in hypnosis, but since the other forms of treatment he had tried (years of psychoanalysis, behavior therapy, marital therapy, etc.) had been unsuccessful, Bill asked Mark to give it a try. Bill did a bit of hypnosis in the first session, but Mark looked very uncomfortable, moving around and tensing his facial muscles throughout the process. He wasn't impressed with the results but was willing to give it another try.

During their next appointment, Bill did a 40-minute hypnosis session with Mark. For about 15 minutes during that trance, Mark was symptom-free—and continued that way for about two hours afterward. Even though Mark still wasn't convinced in hypnosis, and didn't entirely believe he had been in trance, something seemed to help.

By the next session, Mark told Bill what had gone on for him during the previous trances (or pseudotrances, since he didn't believe he'd been in one). Mark said he would have his obsessions, get tense, lose the meanings of words, and begin to dwell on the idea that there would not be enough time for him to go into trance. So Bill began, using inclusion and permission, "Okay, for this trance you can keep your eyes open, or you can close your eyes." Mark closed his eyes, as he usually did, and Bill said, "And as you're sitting there, I already know that you may be thinking you are not going to be able to go into trance, because we have talked too long and we don't have enough time now to do it. So you can think that, that's okay. You may be thinking that this trance stuff is a bunch of junk. And you can think that, that's okay. You may be distracted by one of your symptoms, maybe by the tension in your jaw and your neck. You may think you're too tense to go into trance, and that's okay. You can be tense and you can still go into trance, or you could relax. But you don't have to relax to go into trance. You can be thinking, wondering, how I'm coming up with the words that I'm coming up with and analyzing the words and sentences that I'm saying, and that's okay. You might be worried about the Big Stutter, and that's okay. You can just let yourself feel what you feel, think what you think, experience what you're experiencing and not think what you don't think, not experience what you don't experience and not feel what you don't feel, and you can continue to go into trance."

At that point, Mark popped his eyes open. He said, "That's why I come here."

"So, you believe in trance now?"

Mark replied, "No, no. I still think the hypnosis is a bunch of junk. I come here to hear those words you just said. That's what helps me."

Bill said, "What do you mean?"

Mark said, "In some way, somehow, during the first couple of minutes of this thing that you call hypnosis, for a brief period of time I can't do anything wrong. It's the only time in my life when I can't do anything wrong. So you can skip this hypnosis stuff, but keep doing the stuff you are doing at the beginning of the hypnosis, because that's what is helping me."

That crystallized for Bill what he had been doing with many people, especially those who had been abused. Their inner experience was often one of feeling that something (or everything) they were doing was somehow wrong. Having *all* of their experience validated and included was a very powerful intervention.

We first learned this from doing hypnosis in the tradition of Milton Erickson. People who seek hypnosis often have weird ideas about what it is like, what will happen during it, or what will be required of them to enter trance. Among other things, they believe that they must be relaxed to go into trance, that they won't hear anything that the hypnotist says or any noises around them, or that they will be knocked out.

Although none of those features are essential for experiencing trance, many people define hypnosis in this small circle, tightly bound by musts and can'ts. What the hypnotist must do is make a bigger circle and take the pressure off people so that they don't have to have these experiences or so that they can just allow these experiences without having to force them.

So we say, "You don't have to be relaxed, and you can relax. You can listen to or hear everything that I say, or you don't have to. You may remember what I say, and you may not remember. You don't have to believe anything about this."

We just start to unhook them from the necessities or the impossibilities. We remove the pressure that they put on themselves by valuing and validating everything about their experience, even the opposite of what they think they need to be doing at the moment. Perhaps they're thinking: "I need to relax. My jaws are tense."

The first thing we do is value that tension, value their being there at that moment. The second thing we do is give the possibility of it not being there. So we might say, "You can notice the tension in your jaw, you can have tension in your jaw or your neck or your throat and you don't have to be tense. You may relax, but you don't have to relax and you can go into trance, even if you aren't relaxed."

Even when we don't do trancework, we've found that this cross-validating is of enormous benefit, particularly for clients who have been abused or traumatized.

ACKNOWLEDGMENT AND POSSIBILITY: THE MUTANT CHILD OF CARL ROGERS AND MILTON ERICKSON

Bill's first job in the field was as a half-time telephone suicide crisis worker and half-time outpatient therapist. Bob's was as a counselor at an emergency shelter for runaway and homeless youth. This also involved working with a 24-hour crisis hotline. What we discovered in these jobs was that in a few short minutes it was important to establish a connection with the person in crisis and begin the problem-solving process. If this did not happen quickly, they might hang up, leave and get hurt, or try to kill themselves.

With these crisis calls, the dilemma was finding a way of balancing acknowledgment with directive questions. This is precisely what we did. We acknowledged people and their experiences and feelings while asking them straight-ahead questions about their situations, what they needed, and what they wanted to change. Not only did this seem to work for clients, but it provided us with a framework for working with people in crisis.

Ironically, while we were doing this over the phone, we both behaved quite differently with our outpatients. In individual counseling sessions, we simply listened and reflected. In other words, we acknowledged, but we didn't direct. As a result, it seemed to take our clients longer to change. Sometimes they didn't change. Although some clients did respond well to the process of listening, reflecting, and acknowledging, most seemed to need something more. We found that what they needed was a combination of Milton Erickson's possibility-oriented approach and Carl Rogers's empathy and acknowledgment. When Bill studied with Milton Erickson, he learned that Erickson was using a directive approach but was very effective at developing rapport with his clients. He would not just acknowledge, then step back. Instead, Erickson would move into their experience and initiate a search for possibilities. What he was doing resonated with Bill, as he realized that his work was reflecting a kind of combination of Carl Rogers and Milton Erickson. This made Bill a sort of mutant child of the two.

How do you actually acknowledge clients and move toward possibilities at the same time in therapy?

CARL ROGERS WITH A TWIST: INTRODUCING POSSIBILITIES INTO PAST AND PRESENT PROBLEM REPORTS

From Rogers, we learned the importance of empathy and acknowledgment in therapy. We also learned how to become adept at reflecting clients' experiences back to them. But as we mentioned earlier, most clients seem to need more. So what we offer is a twist to the typical idea of pure reflection. Through the language of change, we can assist clients in the opening up of possibilities. We have found three ways of doing this:

1. Reflect back clients' responses or problem reports in the past tense (folks at the White House sometimes refer to this as "spin control"). Here is typically how we do this:

   CLIENT: I'm depressed.

   THERAPIST: So you've been depressed.

   CLIENT: I feel like cutting myself.

   THERAPIST: You've felt like cutting yourself.

   CLIENT: I'm bad.

   THERAPIST: You've felt bad about yourself.

As illustrated, when a client gives a present tense statement of a problem, we acknowledge and reflect back the problem using the past tense. This is not pure Carl Rogers because we are moving beyond reflection. We acknowledge and validate people where they are, but by recasting the problem in the past tense, we introduce the possibility of a different present or future. The subtle linguistic shift to the past tense helps clear the way for the client to move on.

It is important to keep both pieces of the puzzle in mind: reflecting/validation and suggesting possibilities. If you only acknowledge and validate, some people will move on, but most will not. Conversely, if you simply stress that people *should* move on, they may well hear that as invalidation. So, like all progeny, we seek to combine the best of our parents. We have found that this hybrid Rogerian/Ericksonian approach is particularly useful with clients who have been traumatized.

2. Take clients' general statements such as "everything," "everybody," "nobody," "always," and "never" and translate them into partial statements. This can be done by using qualifiers related to time (e.g., recently, in the last while, in the past month or so, most of the time, much of the time), intensity (e.g., a bit less, somewhat more), or partiality (e.g., a lot, some, most, many). We do not seek to minimize clients' experiences or invalidate them. Instead, we want to gently introduce the idea of possibilities:

    CLIENT: I have flashbacks all the time.

    THERAPIST: So you have flashbacks a lot of the time.

    CLIENT: Nothing ever goes right for me.

    THERAPIST: Sometimes it seems like nothing goes right.

    CLIENT: I can't go on.

THERAPIST: Recently, you've been feeling like you're at the end of your rope.

The idea is to go from global to partial while continuing to acknowledge and validate the person. We want to create a little opening where change is possible.

3. Translate clients' statements of truth or reality into perceptual statements or subjective realities:

   CLIENT: I'm a bad person because I was sexually abused.

   THERAPIST: So you've really gotten the idea that you are bad because you were sexually abused.

   CLIENT: I'll never get over this.

   THERAPIST: It seems your abuse has hurt you so much that you'll never heal.

   CLIENT: I'm evil.

   THERAPIST: Your sense is that there is evil in you.

People's statements are not the way things are, but the way they have perceived or experienced a particular thing. By reflecting back their statements as perceptions, we can introduce the notion of possibility.

When acknowledgment and validation are combined with language of change and possibility in ongoing therapist reflections, clients begin to shift their self-perceptions. This process continues throughout the therapy. In time, clients develop a more possibility-oriented sense of themselves.

If the therapist doesn't validate, if the process feels like a minimization, or if clients feel pushed to move on, they will react. They will say things like:

CLIENT: Not most of the time! All the time!

THERAPIST: Okay. You've really felt bad about yourself all the time.

If the person reacts this way, we are not getting it right. We want to validate them and introduce possibility—*You've really felt bad about yourself all the time.* These are subtle linguistic shifts, invitations, not coercions or judgments and the voice of society that says, "Move on!" or "Get over it!" Clients have usually heard enough of that type of talk, which generally translates to invalidation and blame for them. So we are not trying to dissuade anyone out of their perceptions and experiences. Instead, we want to offer up the idea that even though their world has been overwhelming and painful, change is possible:

Bill was consulting on a case in which the client, Claire, had been doing two years of regressive, cathartic-type work to resolve her history of sexual abuse. Claire, who had been making good progress, asked him if he could help her with some troubling incidents that had occurred over the past few weeks. One was that she was riding her horse when all of a sudden, she had absolutely no idea how to ride a horse. Claire knew intellectually that she knew how to ride, but she could not remember in her body. As they were discussing what had happened, Bill asked the woman to describe the pattern that had led up to the incident. She told him that it felt like a wave, which started at her feet and began to move up through her body. As Claire described the wave, she began to experience it. Bill suggested that she could find a way to stay oriented to the present or to change the pattern, but the wave came on anyway. Since it was happening automatically, Bill suggested that rather than fight it, Claire cooperate with the experience. As she did, she began to experience the sensation of being raped. Claire spoke of a hunting trip her father had taken her on, during which he had raped her in a cold cabin in the woods. She was quite terrified as she "relived" the experience. Claire became so frightened that she told Bill that she had to jump into her "black hole." Bill told her that that was fine. Once inside her black hole, she reported that she was safe, because in the hole she couldn't feel anything or see anything. It was as if she didn't exist. Bill said that was fine and told her to remain where she was and to keep moving. She replied that she couldn't keep moving, as there was nobody there and nowhere to go. Bill repeated that she could be right where she was and she could keep moving. To her surprise, she said she saw a light in front of her. She had been in this black hole many times and had never had this experience. Bill asked her if it was all right to go toward the light. She said it was, and began moving in that direction. As she came closer, she reported that the light was coming from a room that was warm and safe— very different from that cold cabin from which she had just escaped. She went inside and found an alternate safe place to the black hole. In this one place, she could see, hear, and be.

How did Bill know there would be a way out of the black hole that led to a safe room? He didn't, but he trusted that if he acknowledged and supported her where she was, and then invited her to move in the direction of change and new possibilities, something would emerge. That is our faith and our experience. If you just acknowledge people, they will feel accepted and validated, but they may not move on. With both acknowledgment and possibility, they are much more likely to move on more quickly.

ACKNOWLEDGMENT, VALUING, AND VALIDATION

Throughout this chapter, we have focused on bringing together dichotomies and polarities through acknowledgment, validation, and inclusion. There are six components to this valuing:

1. *Acknowledgment.* This involves letting people know that their experience, points of view, and actions have been heard and noted. One can do this by reflecting back to clients, without interpretation, what they said.

2. *Validation.* We let people know that their experiences are valid. They are not bad, weird, sick, or crazy for being who they are and experiencing what they may. And, other people have experienced the same or similar things.

3. *Valuing.* We value both people and their experience. There is a crucial distinction here, though. We let people know that some of their *actions* are valued (e.g., ethical actions that lead toward their goals), and some are not (e.g., physical violence). We seek to value *internal experience* but not harmful actions. So we might say, "It's okay to feel like cutting yourself, and it's not okay to cut yourself." In the realm of action there are going to be things that are okay and not okay. However, we want to value everything in the realm of experience and who the person is.

4. *Permission.* This includes permission "to" and permission "not to have to." We might say, "It's okay to feel angry, and you don't have to feel angry." We want people to know it is okay to feel what they are feeling. Their feelings represent who they are.

5. *Inclusion.* This involves including whatever the person has excluded or thrown out. To do this, we want to use the word "and," not "but." We might say, "You can want to go to the beach, and you can go to work" or "You can feel like cutting yourself and not cut yourself." There is no contradiction present. It can all be included in their experience.

6. *Accountability.* We acknowledge and validate people's experiences, but at the same time, we hold them accountable for their actions. They can feel pain and want to retaliate or hurt themselves or someone else, and not do the harmful behavior.

These precepts may seem basic, but we strongly believe that if people don't feel acknowledged and validated from the beginning they will not move on past the traumas and toward change—what we call "PossibilityLand." But acknowledging and validating must be accompanied by other techniques aimed at opening possibilities.

DEVELOPING A RELATIONSHIP WITH DISSOCIATED, DEVALUED, AND DISOWNED ASPECTS OF SELF

The following story indicates the basic components or steps to having people begin to value and move toward their devalued experiences:

There is a book called A Wizard of Earthsea, by Ursula K. Le Guin (1968), that is part of a series. It gives a template for how to embrace what has been disowned and devalued.

It is fantasy, a story about a kid who grows up in this world where wizardry is a greatly admired skill. Wizards

*can change the weather, so the crops can grow a little better.
They can heal people. Wizards know all these wonderful skills.
They are the keepers of wisdom and knowledge on this planet.*

   *The story begins when a kid is born into a poor goatherding
family, and he is born with the gift. He discovers, and the vil-
lage comes to realize, that he is really good at this wizardry
stuff, just naturally. A master wizard in the area hears of the
kid's reputation for psychic and healing abilities, seeks him out,
and offers to take him on as his apprentice. The kid accepts,
but soon surpasses even his mentor's knowledge and skill. The
master wizard convinces the reluctant boy that he must to go to
the central wizard school on a faraway island because he has
a great gift that can be best furthered in that special place.*

   *He goes there at age 13 and he is a child prodigy, but there
is an older, former child prodigy, who never really developed
as well as he might have because he was a bit spoiled (being a
prince and used to having others do his work for him). This
older boy is jealous of this new kid on the block. So, they develop
a rivalry. The older one teases, tortures, and hassles the
younger one, until finally, one day the younger one, feeling his
growing power and sure he can best his older rival, challenges
the older one to a duel of sorcery.*

   *The older one accepts and says to the younger one, "If you
are so great, how about you raise someone from the dead.
Even the greatest wizards can barely do that. You can't do
that!"*

   "Yeah, I can!" the younger one says.

   *So they go outside the wizard school walls to a place of
power and the young wizard raises someone from the dead.
Now, you're not supposed to do this (it's against the Wizard
Code of Ethics), and he finds that he cannot contain the energy. As he raises the spirit from the dead, there is a big crack
of lightning, and he gets attacked by the power he has un-
leashed with his Spell of Summoning. Terrible things happen in*

*the whole vicinity and the head wizard must come and save
him, contain the energy, and rebury the spirit.*

*The young wizard passes out. But before he loses con-
sciousness, he sees this dark mass slithering from an opening,
a ripped opening in the fabric of the world, that he called. He
sees it, but he doesn't understand it.*

*For four weeks, he's in a coma and they don't know if he
will live or die. He's blind, deaf, and mute, though at times he
cries out like an animal. Slowly, the healing begins; they nurse
him back to health, but he is terribly ashamed that he has be-
trayed the trust the wizards have put in him. He has shamed
the whole wizard community. For months, he can't speak without stammering. He has a scar on his face from the attack. He
begins to feel the presence of that evil dark mass that his failure has loosed on the world. He feels that it hates him and
would destroy him if it could. He eventually completes his
training and decides to leave the school and accepts a small assignment, far below his capabilities. He knows that once he
leaves the school, the wizards there can no longer protect him
from certain attack and possession by the dark shadow, but
he feels as if his life is barely worth living and cares little for
his safety.*

*He goes off and quickly completes his assignment. He begins
to wake up in the middle of the night in a cold sweat, terrified
of this evil that he now knows is stalking him. He panics and
runs, trying to escape what he fears.*

*He moves from town to town, traveling great distances. For
a while, he doesn't feel the evil stalking him anymore. Alas,
soon he feels it coming for him again. It can tell where he is by
psychic connection. He ends up running from place to place
in an attempt to hide, but there is no safe place.*

*Finally, he decides that he has brought this evil thing into the
world and his life is worthless. In desperation, he seeks advice
from his first teacher and after talking with him, realizes what*

he must do. He will become the hunter and attempt to kill this thing. He knows that it may overcome him, but he might just be able to kill it because he does have some skills. He lets the thing come closer and closer even though he is totally terrified. Suddenly, the dark thing is upon him and he turns around to fight it to the death. But an unexpected thing happens. As he goes toward the black thing, he feels a shift in the energy and the black thing says, "Uh-oh!" turns around and starts to run away. It says, "I'm getting out of here!"

So he has to chase the black thing all through the world by boat until he finally comes to the end of the world. He chases it until it appears as an illusion. The open sea all of a sudden becomes dry land and there it is. The wizard and the shadow walk toward each other, the shadow changing form as they get closer and closer. He reaches out to take hold of the shadow and it becomes his shadow, his dark self—and wouldn't you know, as soon as he touches it, it goes inside, he incorporates it, they become one, and he is healed and whole again. He goes on, now as a powerfully whole person, to become the head wizard, a very wise and humble man indeed.

That story captures the idea that we've been talking about. People have been dissociating, devaluing, disowning; and what we have to do is get them to turn around and start to face whatever has been chasing them. We invite people into relationship with aspects of themselves that they have been trying to get rid of. They can then begin to value what was dissociated, devalued, and disowned. For some people, this is a gradual, step-by-step process. Here are some of the steps we have observed people taking:

1. *Acknowledging the existence of the aspect or experience.*
    In this initial phase, the person takes note of the experience, perception, or aspect previously dissociated,

disowned, and devalued. The person acknowledges that the aspect can exist. For example, he or she might say, "I can feel anger sometimes." The person does not have to like the aspect, but acknowledges that it can be present.

2. *Developing a respectful relationship or dialogue with the aspect or experience.* This step moves beyond mere acknowledgment and represents some type of connection between the person and aspect of self. It may involve writing, drawing, inner or outer dialogue, or any other method that allows for the person and his or her experience to start to communicate on a respectful and mutual basis.

3. *Making room for the aspect or experience. Allowing it to exist within the boundaries of self.* In this situation, a person who has acknowledged that an aspect or experience can exist continues to move toward it and make room for it. Instead of trying to get rid of or suppress the experience or aspect, the person gives it permission to exist within the experience or self.

4. *Valuing the aspect or experience.* The person moves away from the idea that an aspect or experience is bad, evil, unnecessary, or negative in general. The consideration is that the aspect or experience may actually be good, valuable, helpful, or useful in some way that was previously unnoticed.

5. *Embracing the aspect or experience.* The person continues to move beyond the toleration or allowance of an aspect or experience, and may actually pursue and embrace it.

6. *Incorporating the aspect or experience.* The realization develops in the person, not just intellectually but

experientially, that the aspect or experiences is *the self.* This means the person experiences "it" in the body, and a kind of integration occurs.

Janet had been angry for months. She was afraid, however, that her rage would be so out of control that it would damage her husband and children and others who came in contact with her, so she kept a tight clamp on those angry feelings. After we discussed the stance of just letting your feelings be the way they are, she decided to experiment with that idea. One weekend, her husband and older son went out of town for the weekend, and she was at home with her 12-year-old. She decided to give herself permission to get into her anger and rage, but set the limit that she wouldn't show any of it to her son, who was in and out of the house all weekend. She was amazed to discover that she wasn't "out of control" when she felt the rage, rather that she felt, in a strange way, more in control. All weekend, she indulged in angry fantasies and rageful imagined conversations with her husband and others with whom she was angry. "The anger just came and went all weekend, sometimes it was very strong and sometimes it was almost totally gone," she reported. By the end of the weekend, she had a different sense of the anger—it just didn't run the show anymore like it used to.

In this book, we talk about ways of acknowledging the details of what happened in the abuse without reliving them as a way to validate. In addition, if people do regress, there are ways not to invalidate them. We liken this approach to the sport of *curling,* which is played on ice with a stone and four members on two separate teams. The object is to slide the stone down the ice toward a target circle. As the stone is sliding, the team members sweep in front of it to smooth the ice so it goes further. They also sweep in certain directions to assist the stone on its path to the target circle.

This is what we are trying to do with acknowledgment and validation. We want to sweep in front of clients as we watch and listen to them. If we don't do that, it is as if we're doing techniques on them. We see ourselves as being with people, asking where they are and what they see happening. We are reflecting that back to them and sweeping open possibilities for the present and the future.

When invited, most people do begin to experience life in a way that is present and future oriented, rather than a repetition of the painful past. People can get through their traumas a lot quicker, and therapy can be a lot more focused and less disruptive to their lives.

In the next chapter, we examine another method of getting people moving.

SUMMARY POINTS
CHAPTER TWO

❖ One method of getting people who are stuck in rep-
etitious experience moving again is to validate what
they have invalidated or devalued and invite them to
include what they have disowned.

❖ Trance logic is a type of experience in which seemingly contradictory ideas, experiences, or facets of a
person can be experienced simultaneously.

❖ The Inclusive Self has the ability to use trance logic
to help trauma survivors revalue and include seemingly conflicted aspects of their lives.

❖ It is important to both validate and invite people
into new possibilities.

CHAPTER THREE

Strong at the Broken Places

DISRUPTING PROBLEM PATTERNS AND
EVOKING SOLUTION PATTERNS
AND CONTEXTS

BILL SAW A WOMAN, Phyllicia, who had been abused as a child. As a result, she frequently had waves of compelling suicidal feelings sweep over her. "It's like somebody shoots me in the ass with instant suicidal impulses. It's all I can do not to drive my car into a concrete barrier on the highway when this comes over me," she said. Bill asked what had helped her not drive into the barriers. Phyllicia said that thinking about the impact it would have on her 14-year-old daughter was one thing. The other thing was that she had decided to get some counseling. Bill asked Phyllicia what she thought the counseling might do for her. Just talking to someone was helpful, she said, and getting out of her usual perspective by hearing someone else's. Phyllicia went on to discuss some of the problems she had that added into the suicidal impulses.

She had come out as a lesbian after many years in an unhappy marriage. During sex with various female partners since then, she would get to the same point again and again. She would begin to have sex and then find herself growing bored midway through the act. Her mind would just drift away. Soon she would break up with that partner and search for someone more interesting. After repeating the pattern with several partners, though, she began to despair of ever finding someone to stay with. She would then become very depressed about this, which would provoke her "instant suicidal injections" shortly thereafter.

Bill asked if there were times when Phyllicia had experienced better sex with women. Phyllicia said that a few times she had spoken up to her partners, told them she was bored, and explained that she would prefer some other kinds of sexual stimulation. On those occasions, the partners had responded, and Phyllicia was able to get more enjoyment from the sex that followed. Bill told her it sounded like speaking her truth was a solution in several situations. She had begun to speak her truth when she first realized she was gay. This had led to the relief of a great deal of confusion and sadness. She used to get up after sex with her husband and go into the bathroom and cry silently. She had no idea why she did this until she finally realized she was not interested in having sex with men. She felt great relief when she had finally spoken to others about her abuse. Then, finally, she was able to sustain a sexual and romantic relationship with a woman longer during the times she had spoken up about her sexual experience and interests. Once she realized this, she started making plans for areas in which she could speak up and tell her truth. Her feelings of suicidality diminished greatly as she followed these plans.

A MAP OF PROBLEMLAND: IDENTIFYING AND DISRUPTING PROBLEM PATTERNS

As mentioned in Chapter One, before delving into the specifics of any complaint, we want to be clear on what the complaint is. What brought the person to therapy? After getting an initial sense of what is bothering the person, we begin to elicit more detailed information. What we are seeking is patterns. To find the patterns, we must get descriptions of what the person is doing that constitutes or accompanies the problem. Descriptions are different from theories or conclusions. We have referred to this process as getting people to use *videotalk* (O'Hanlon & Wilk, 1987); that is, getting people to describe their problem so it can be seen and heard as if on a videotape. Another way of describing videotalk is as the "doing" of the problem.

We might ask a person to describe to us the "doing" of self-mutilation. When does the person typically hurt herself? How does the person start to hurt herself? What kinds of implements does she use to hurt herself, if any? What parts of her body does she typically hurt? What parts does she never hurt?

Even if the complaint is about something internal, you can still elicit a description of the "doing" that accompanies it. For example, you could ask, "When you are having your flashbacks, what would someone who is watching you at that moment see differently from other moments when there are no flashbacks?" Or, "What do you typically do when you get depressed?" Focusing on the doing helps isolate the problem.

What is a problem? From our perspective, a therapeutically addressable problem:

❖ Must occur repetitively.

❖ Must be distinguished and attended to.

❖ Must be valued negatively (as bad, wrong, sick, crazy, evil, shameful, unacceptable, intolerable).

❖ Must be considered to be involuntary in at least some aspect.

Milton Erickson was fascinated with clients' problems and symptoms and the way they did them. He would ask clients to describe in minute detail the particulars of their problem. He would ask questions about:

❖ How the problem occurred.

❖ Where the problem occurred.

❖ With whom the problem occurred.

❖ How often the problem occurred (frequency).

❖ How long the problem occurred (duration).

Essentially, he wanted to map out the details of the problem. Erickson would focus on the problem so intently it was almost as if he was studying the person in order to play that role in a movie.

We share Erickson's curiosity. We explore with clients the negative problem patterns that seem to be inhibiting or intruding in their lives. We seek to be geographers, exploring the topography and coastline of Problem-Land. We want to know the details of the problem or symptom, *and* help the client to find ways of escaping it. By isolating the problem, we can intervene in the patterns that make up the problem, or to change the contexts around the problem so they no longer contain the problem or symptom (O'Hanlon, 1982, 1987; O'Hanlon & Weiner-Davis, 1989; O'Hanlon & Wilk, 1987;).

Clients' descriptions of the problems help us understand what they mean by the words they use, so we don't impose so much of our own interpretations on those words. In addition, what we are searching for is any aspect of the problem that repeats or indicates a pattern. Here are some ways we have found, following Erickson's example, to ferret out the patterns of the problem:

❖ How often does the problem typically happen (once an hour, once a day, once a week)?

❖ Find the typical timing (time of day, time of week, time of month, time of year) of the problem.

❖ Find the duration of the problem (how long it typically lasts).

❖ Where does the problem typically happen?

❖ What does the person and others who are around usually do when the problem is happening?

Once we recognize a problematic pattern, we can then begin to find ways of disrupting it or replacing it with a solution pattern.

CHANGING PROBLEM PATTERNS

We typically suggest changes in the problem pattern after we have enough details about the pattern to get a sense of the possibilities for a noticeable change that would be within the person's power to bring about. Usually this involves changing actions, which may include:

❖ The sequence.

❖ The antecedents.

❖ The consequences.

❖ Invariant actions.

❖ Repetitive interactions.

❖ Body behavior.

Yvonne Dolan has recounted several creative tasks she and clients have come up with to change patterns of self-mutilation that often trouble abuse survivors. In one case, Yvonne learned that the client's sight of her own blood after she cut her arm was what soothed her when she was upset. They did an experiment and the client found that painting red lipstick (or Mercurochrome, for those of you who are old enough to remember that) on her arm had the same soothing effect. In another case, Yvonne worked with an artist who was cutting herself and they found that the artist could turn the impulse to cut into an artistic project. The client stretched a big canvas and made gigantic slash marks with her paintbrush on the canvas every time she felt the urge to cut. This greatly decreased the frequency and severity of the cutting.

The location or setting in which the problem typically happens can also be the focus of change:

A woman who was depressed and isolated, feeling that she could trust no one after the abuse she had suffered, agreed to go to a coffeehouse when she got very desperate. She did not have to talk to anyone, but just to sit there for at least two hours. She began to go to the coffeehouse nightly because she was usually depressed. After a time, she became a familiar face, and the staff of the coffeehouse began to engage her in conversation. She made a few friends and began to volunteer at the coffeehouse helping book the musical acts they had decided to add to the atmosphere.

One can also suggest changes in the timing (frequency, time of occurrence, duration) of the problem:

Martha, an abuse survivor, spent a good portion of her evening picking at her fingernails until they bled. Martha tried to stop this behavior, but she found it so compelling that she couldn't avoid it. The therapist suggested that Martha try an experiment and schedule 15-minute picking sessions each night. Martha found that, during the nonscheduled times, the compulsion was gone because she knew she had her scheduled time to engage in the habit. Martha found herself doing more productive and interesting things with her evenings. Occasionally, she even forgot to pick her nails.

Another option is to suggest changes in the nonverbals (voice tones, gestures, body movements, eye contact, etc.) around the problem:

Jenny was having trouble with her eating disorder (bulimia) during social occasions when food was present. Normally a very sociable person, she had almost decided to stop attending any social gathering that might have food. She would become so focused on the food during these gatherings (avoiding it, fearing that everyone would know she was compulsively eating) that she would have a terrible time. She would slink about the party, head down, avoiding any contact or conversation with anyone. Sometimes she would binge and sometimes not, but the experience was unpleasant regardless. Together with Bill, she devised a plan to change the pattern. The next party she attended, she agreed to go up to at least three people, look them in the eye, and introduce herself, before she began to focus on the food. When she carried out the plan, she found she became so absorbed in the conversations she was having that food became a nonissue.

INVITATION TO SOLUTIONLAND: IDENTIFYING, EVOKING, AND USING SOLUTION PATTERNS

In addition to (or instead of) changing problem patterns, we seek to elicit and evoke previous solution patterns, including abilities, competencies, and strengths. The idea is not to convince clients they have solutions and competences, but to ask questions and gather information in a way that highlights these possibilities for them. The emphasis is on evoking a sense of competence and an experience of being able to solve problems. Often when clients become caught up in their problematic patterns, they do not recall the wealth of experience they have available. We search in various areas to find this sense of competence and to identify previously successful strategies for dealing with or resolving the particular problems the client has brought to therapy. The following techniques are useful for gathering information about solutions and evoking them:

❖ *Find out about previous solutions to the problem, including partial solutions and partial successes.* Ask clients to detail times when they expected the problem, but did not experience it. For example, you might ask, "From what we understand, usually you would have just backed down in the face of intimidation like that, but you didn't that one time. What did you do that was different this time? How did you get yourself to do it?" Or, "You didn't cut yourself as much last night. How did you keep yourself from doing what you usually have done? What did you do this time instead of continuing to cut?"

❖ *Find out what happens as the problem ends or starts to end.* What is the first sign the client has that the problem is going away or subsiding? How can the person's friends, family, coworkers, etc., tell when the problem has subsided or started to subside? What will the person be doing when the problem has ended or subsided? How do these problem-free activities differ from what the client does when the problem is happening or present? Is there anything the person or significant others have noticed that helps the problem subside more quickly?

Some sample questions to help elicit this information include: "So when you stop cutting, how do you know it's time to stop? What cues do you notice that tell you are winding down or are going to stop? Then, what do you start doing as you finish the cutting?" Or, "When the sexual compulsion starts to diminish and you are not feeling so compelled to go out and have sex with strangers, what do you start focusing on and doing?"

❖ *Find out about any helpful changes that have happened before treatment began.* Sometimes therapists don't give their clients enough credit. At times, clients may have already begun solving the problem before they seek help. Just focusing on the problem enough to seek therapy can help clients make changes. It may be that the sense that they will get some help gives them enough hope and energy to begin making changes. In a way, also, therapy can have a kind of "flossing" effect—clients begin to direct more attention and effort to the problem—similar to the way we floss more vigorously or often before a visit to the dentist. Asking about positive pretreatment changes of this sort can yield important information about how people solve their problems or make changes.

❖ *Search for contexts in which the person feels competent and has good problem-solving or creative skills.* These contexts may include hobbies or job skills. You might also identify situations in which the problem would not occur (e.g., at work, in a restaurant). Find out about times when the person or someone he or she knows has faced a similar problem and resolved it in a way that he or she liked.

❖ *Ask why the problem isn't worse.* Have the client explain, compared with the worst possible state a person could be in, why the problem isn't that severe. This normalizes and helps put things in perspective and gives you information about how clients restrain themselves from getting into worse trouble. Another way to do this is to ask the client to compare any incident of the problem to the worst manifestation and explain what is different about the times the problem is less severe.

Wendy Kaminer (1992, pp. 81–85) tells a poignant story of a discovery she made about trauma survivors. In writing a book about 12-step and self-help groups, she attended hundreds of meetings. In her view, most of the self-help meetings were characterized by self-pitying and endlessly visiting of the group participants' traumatic childhood experiences. In the midst of her research, however, she visited a group of Cambodian women, survivors of the killing fields; most of them had experienced and seen untold horrors and death, from which they had fled to this new and strange country. Kaminer was struck by the contrast between the Cambodian women's group and the self-help groups she was researching. The Cambodians spoke little about the past and spent much of their time helping each other learn practical things that could help them in their everyday lives: more English phrases, the local bus system, and so on. They joked and laughed a great deal. Only once, when news came on the radio of a similar massacre that had recently occurred in another country, did the women express sadness. They all got quiet, spoke a little about their painful experiences, then quickly moved back into their usual pattern of searching for solutions rather than dwelling on problems.

The approach we are detailing in this chapter is similar to the strategy used by these women. Cambodian women did not emulate what many American trauma survivors do in self-help groups. We encourage people who are haunted by trauma to move on from its effects by changing their patterns, not by rehashing or reliving their traumatic experiences.

INTERRUPTING MUTUAL SYMPTOMATIC
TRANCE INDUCTION: COUPLES THERAPY

One could think about these pattern interventions, whether breaking up the problem patterns or evoking and using solution patterns, as ways to wake up clients from symptomatic trance. Since symptomatic trance involves repetition and repetition can be trance-inducing (think of the hypnotist's repetitive suggestions), changing the repetitive patterns can break up the trance and wake people up.

In identifying and changing problem patterns (symptomatic trances), there seems to be no more fertile ground than intimate relationships. People can trigger each other into "bad" trances (symptomatic states) during which one or both partners "go on automatic." They lose contact with their resources, feel dissociated, and behave in an incongruent manner. Couples often develop communication and interaction patterns that trigger each other's bad trance. Typical patterns include communications that blame, invalidate, close down possibilities, or contain vague/ambiguous language. Sometimes, all it takes is a nonverbal signal or a certain kind of touch to cue off a symptomatic trance.

We use three techniques to aid couples to avoid these bad trances:

1. Help them use videotalk and stop trying to analyze, change, or fix each other's insides.
2. Change patterns of actions between the two of them.

3. Help them orient to the present time, place, and person to wake them up from the bad trance in which they are bringing the past vividly or repetitively into the present.

USING VIDEOTALK

In several of Bill's previous publications (Hudson & O'Hanlon, 1992; O'Hanlon & Hudson, 1996; O'Hanlon & Wilk, 1987), he has detailed a way of helping couples bypass blaming and misunderstandings that come about because we all can have different meanings for the same abstract words. This involves coaching couples to speak to each other in videotalk (i.e., descriptive, sensory-based words and phrases rather than vague or interpretive words and phrases). The couple doesn't need to do this all the time, only in areas in which they usually experience bad, or symptomatic, trance. This seems especially important for people who have suffered sexual abuse traumas because they are typically very sensitized to being intruded on. Many of the problematic patterns that occur in couples' communication involve what Virginia Satir called "mind reading." This is when one person attributes motives to another or tells the other what he or she is thinking or feeling. Videotalk avoids this by having couples focus their comments to each other on what they can observe, rather than what they infer or attribute.

CHANGING RELATIONSHIP PATTERNS

A couple entered therapy complaining about sexual problems. The wife had been sexually abused as a child and had begun experiencing flashbacks during sex. When the patterns of their sexual interactions were investigated, it became clear that there were some times when their sex life was not intruded on by the flashbacks and other times when the flashbacks were problematic and intrusive. Close tracking of the differences between the two types of interactions revealed that when the husband did anything to "restrain" his wife, such as holding her hand while having intercourse, it precipitated a flashback. As soon as they realized this, they changed their lovemaking patterns to ensure that the husband did nothing that reminded the wife of being restrained, as she had been when she was abused.

Something about the couple's current interaction reminds one or both of previous painful or shameful times. Investigating the patterns around and involved in the problem can offer many places to change the patterns. Creative experimentation can bypass the cues for bad trance.

REORIENT PEOPLE TO THE PRESENT TIME, PLACE, AND PERSON

One time while Bill was walking down the hall at the mental health center, the medical director asked him if he would deliver a message to one of the therapists, Jane, who also worked part-time in administration. Bill said he'd be glad to. On his way back to his office, he stopped by Jane's office and told her that Dr. Holmes had said to tell her that the meeting tomorrow was canceled. On hearing this, Jane became livid and began yelling at Bill, telling him how he was like all the other "goddam hypocritical power-hungry men" she had ever known. Bill was so amazed at this outburst, he didn't even take it personally. He just stood and listened for a few minutes until he finally interrupted Jane and said, "Jane, I don't know who you're upset with, but it's not me!" Jane seemed to come to her senses, calmed down, and embarassedly apologized. "I'm sorry, Bill. You're right, it isn't you. You see, they have promised me a promotion and it was to be announced at the meeting tomorrow, but I've been getting the sense that they are going to break their promise to me. My ex-husband used to play the same kind of games with me, promising me the moon to get me to do whatever he wanted and then never following through."

She had been seeing her ex-husband's face superimposed on Bill's. When Bill interrupted her, she reoriented to the present to see who was really in front of her. People who have been abused are often bringing their past with them and projecting the past traumas on the present person or place. One way to invite them out of this past bad trance is to have them attend to the present through their sensory experience:

A couple was experiencing problems with their sex life since the husband had begun to remember being raped by a priest when he was a child. What finally worked for them was to have the husband turn on the lights if he began to have uncomfortable experiences while they were having sex. He was then to look closely at his partner's face, touching it and asking her to say some words. In this way, he was able to come back to the present and realize that his wife was with him having loving sex, rather than that he was being raped by that priest from long ago.

Yvonne Dolan (1991) has a method of bringing people out of flashbacks. As soon as the flashback begins, she suggests that they begin to pay attention to at least five things that they can see in the present environment, then to attend to five things they can hear in the current environment, five things they can touch, and so on. This seems to bring the person out of that internal, past-reviving unchanging reality into the less threatening, ever-changing external reality.

Much of what we have detailed here can apply to any relationship, whether it be work, friendship, or family.

SUMMARY POINTS
CHAPTER THREE

❖ Repetitive patterns can serve to constantly recreate a traumatic past in the present.

❖ This method of getting people moving involves getting them to describe their problem in action terms (videotalk), discovering and altering repetitive patterns of actions.

❖ There are two ways of altering the problem patterns:

1. Suggest alterations in the typical repetitive actions involved in or contexts surrounding the problem.

2. Elicit and encourage the use of solution patterns; that is, actions that have happened instead of the problem in the typical problem-inducing situation.

❖ Since repetitive interaction patterns in relationships often trigger symptomatic trances, changing these interactions can help bring both partners out of their old unworkable patterns.

❖ Getting couples to use action talk can bypass blame and confusing communications that can induce symptomatic trance.

CHAPTER
FOUR

Spinning the Future

THE VIKTOR FRANKL STRATEGY

*I*N 1990, VIKTOR FRANKL *delivered the keynote address at the second "Evolution of Psychotherapy" conference, in Anaheim, California. As 7,000 people listened, Dr. Frankl told the compelling story of his life. He described the terrible things that had happened to him while he was imprisoned in a Nazi death camp and how he had nearly died many times. He was physically and psychologically abused and tortured. During this plenary session, Dr. Frankl described one day in particular that seemed to be etched deeply within him.*

On a wintry day in Poland, he was being marched through a field with a group of other prisoners. He was dressed in thin clothing, with no socks on, and holes in his shoes. Still very ill from malnutrition and mistreatment, he began to cough. The cough was so severe that he fell to his knees. A guard came over and told him to get moving. He could not even answer because his cough was so intense and debilitating. The guard began to beat him with a club, and told him that he would be left to die if he did not get up. Dr. Frankl knew this was true as he had witnessed it before. Sick, in pain, and being hit, he thought, "This is it for me." He didn't have the wherewithal to get up.

He lay on the ground in no condition to move on. Suddenly, he was no longer there. Instead, he found himself standing at a lectern in postwar Vienna giving a lecture on "The Psychology of Death Camps" before an audience of 200 people, rapt with attention. This lecture is one that he had worked on the whole time he was in the death camp. He talked about the psychological factors behind dehumanization. He then described why, in his view, some people seemed to survive the experience psychologically and emotionally better than others. It is a brilliant lecture, all in his mind's eye and ear. He is no longer in the field (he's dissociated) but is vividly involved in the lecture. During the lecture, he told the imaginary audience about the day Viktor Frankl was in that field being beaten and was certain he didn't have the strength to get up and keep walking. Then, exactly at the moment he was describing to his imaginary audience finally being able to stand up and start walking, his body stood up in the field. The guard stopped beating him and he began to walk. Haltingly at first, then with more strength. He continued to imagine this lecture all the while he was doing the work detail and through the cold march back to the death camp. He collapsed into his bunk, imagining this brilliantly clear speech ending and him getting a standing ovation. Many years later and thousands of miles away, in 1990 in Anaheim, California, he received a standing ovation from 7,000 after his speech.

What did Viktor Frankl do differently from what most people do who have been sexually abused? He dissociated just as most abuse victims do. As previously discussed, that's a pretty good response to trauma. But, instead of staying frozen in time at that moment and repeating it again and again, he created a vision and a sense of a future with possibilities and meaning. He imagined a future that was different from the past; a future in which things worked out. That future vision became so compelling to him that he *had* to get up and walk. If he hadn't, he never would have given that brilliant speech. He had connected with the future. Now he had to take some actions that would get him to the future he knew was waiting for him. To get there, the first order of business was getting up off the ground and starting to walk.

That is what's missing from many clients who have been sexually abused; a really well articulated and good connection to a future with possibilities. Our mission is to help clients do what Viktor Frankl did by rehabilitating and creating a sense of a future where things are different and possible. Some people will have some sense of that possibility-filled future, and we can help them to rehabilitate it and begin to move powerfully toward it. Others have no sense of it and may need to begin to imagine that it is possible to have a future that is different from the past or better than the past.

When clients are able to envision themselves in a preferred future where the trauma is not interfering, the "stuckness" that they are experiencing in the present begins to dissipate. This chapter describes ways to help the client move on from the stuckness. Before delving too deeply into methods for helping people create or rehabilitate possibilities, we need to underscore a crucial distinction: Possibilities shouldn't be confused with positives. People who learn about solution-oriented therapy often say, "I really like this positive approach." This makes us shudder because being positive is sort of like positive thinking. It sends the message, "If you write enough affirmations and just develop the right kind of attitude, you'll be rich (healthy, have a perfect relationship, etc.)." Deepak Chopra has said that trying to think positively often only adds stress to people's lives because it doesn't work for them. We agree; moreover, we would add that if people who have been sexually abused aren't successful at thinking positively, they can be further invalidated and develop a sense that they are incapable or damaged in some way. This may give the message, "See, I can't do anything right. There must be something really wrong with me."

As we look at the world, it doesn't always seem so positive. There's a lot of violence, discrimination, inequities, and terrible things out there. So we are not suggesting that therapists assume a position of being purely positive. We are also wary of a pessimistic or purely negative view (e.g., these clients are permanently damaged by their terrible traumas). Instead, we want to maintain a position that there is pain and there are also possibilities. This view holds, "It's possible, now we have to figure out how to do it":

Bob worked with a woman, Kate, who had been sexually abused by her brother. Kate was regularly told by her mother, "Just don't think about it. And, if you have to think about it just remember that you have a lot going for you. Good things come to those who think good things." Kate became increasingly depressed at being unable to master the ability to think positively, or as she would say, "Think in the right way." During the course of therapy, Kate said that her way of thinking about the abuse was to replay what had happened over and over again. When she tried to think "good things" about her experience, she became depressed and anxious. Thus, she additionally began to feel that she was incompetent at life in general. Bob said, "I think it's interesting that tapes oftentimes have a limited lifetime. If they are played enough times, they eventually become worn out and are replaced by others. Some people gradually replace their old tapes with new ones so it's not such an abrupt change. Others go from 8-tracks to cassettes, for instance, and make a complete change in format. Some old tapes are never replaced because they've gone out of print, or they're just not what the person listens to anymore. It can be a nice thing to be able to decide which tapes to keep and which ones to throw out. I wonder, for you, which tapes would you be interested in keeping and maybe even transferring to CDs, because they last longer?" The woman replied, "You know, one thing I always have playing in my head is the song 'Our House,' you know, 'two cats in the yard, life used to be so hard.' That's what I'd like for myself. A nice cozy place with my fiancé and my cats."

Bob validated Kate's right to play the tapes as long as she wanted to, which counteracted the previous invalidation she received from her mother and her own unsuccessful efforts to "think right."

There's a story about Milton Erickson that also illustrates this point. During a supervision session, a trainee asked, "Dr. Erickson, with all your therapeutic, hypnotic, and strategic skills, do you think you could solve the situation in the Middle East?" Erickson sat there and stared at the floor for a moment, then looked up and said, with a twinkle in his eye, "Bring them to my office." That response captures the essence of this perspective. We want to convey the sense that things can change by inviting people to create futures with possibilities. We don't always have a simple solution, but we always have the sense that something is possible.

THE MOVING WALKWAY: CREATING COMPELLING INVITATIONS INTO POSSIBILITIES

We both travel quite a bit, and our familiarity with airports has led to a healthy relationship with "moving walkways." These conveyor belts take people to their future destinations (gates, baggage carousels, exits, etc.) without the travelers having to do anything. Although most of the people who come to see us are stuck in place, there are ways of interviewing, asking questions, making comments, and telling stories that can have an effect similar to that of the moving walkway. Just as moving walkways transport people toward future destinations, we help clients move toward future possibilities without any conscious effort on their part. Language is our "conveyor belt," and we have three verbal techniques for creating forward momentum:

1. Use words such as "yet" or "so far" to instill a sense of possibility. These words presuppose that even though things feel stuck in the present, at some point in the future things will change. This simple shift in language can help clients create a "light at the end of the tunnel":

    CLIENT: I do better sometimes, but then I slip back.

    THERAPIST: So you haven't quite mastered the ability to stay on course most of the time.

    CLIENT: I'm always depressed.

    THERAPIST: So far you haven't found a way to have meaning in your life yet.

    CLIENT: I was abused. I can't stand myself, so why should anyone else?

    THERAPIST: So you haven't learned to value yourself yet, having gone through that terribly devaluing experience.

2. Recast the problem statement into a statement about the preferred future or goal:

    CLIENT: I think I'm too shy to find a relationship. I'm afraid of women and being rejected.

    THERAPIST: So you'd like to be able to get into a relationship?

    CLIENT: What's the point? I want to kill myself.

    THERAPIST: So you want to find a way that you can know that it's okay to be alive and stay alive?

CLIENT: I've been cutting myself.

THERAPIST: So one of the things that we could do in here is help you find a way to value your body and not hurt yourself?

3. Presuppose changes and progress toward goals by using words like "when" and "will":

    CLIENT: No one wants to be in a relationship with me.

    THERAPIST: So when you get the sense that you have found people who might be interested in having a relationship with you, we'll know we've made some progress.

    CLIENT: I think about the abuse all the time.

    THERAPIST: So as you begin thinking less about the abuse, you'll be doing things you'd rather do with your time.

    CLIENT: I'd like to stop eating compulsively.

    THERAPIST: When you get a handle on your eating, you'll feel better.

In the medical community, there is a growing body of literature on people with chronic illnesses. Findings indicate that people who sense that their pain will end and things will improve have a higher incidence of recovery. Part of what people suffering from the aftereffects of sexual abuse encounter is the notion that they will never be free of the experiences that replay over and over in their minds. Presuppositional language implies that things can change—without minimizing the problems and suffering they are currently experiencing and feeling.

MIRACLES AND CRYSTAL BALLS

There are thousands of documented cases where people who were diagnosed with a chronic or terminal condition have experienced spontaneous recovery. For years, these "miracles" were dismissed as anomalies. One of the commonalties among some of these spontaneous recoveries is patients' perspective that things can change (Chopra, 1989). Again, we are not speaking of a positive attitude, but a sense of a future where the pain no longer exists and their lives are better.

Just as Viktor Frankl envisioned a future where things worked out, we want to help our clients to create that same sense—a time when their lives are free of the suffering that haunts them. Miracles, crystal balls, and videotapes are three techniques that therapists can use with clients to create such futures.

Miracles

One helpful way to help clients to create a vision of the future is to ask them what it would be like if a miracle happened. This concept was developed by Steve de Shazer (1988) as a way to help clients imagine their lives when their problem is solved. Yvonne Dolan (1991) has developed a way to use the miracle question with clients who are suffering from the aftereffects of sexual abuse:

> If a miracle happened in the middle of the night and you had overcome the effects of your childhood abuse to the extent that you no longer needed therapy and felt quite satisfied with your life, what would be different? (p. 34)

This question—or a variation of it—provides a glimpse of how clients might see their future when the therapy is over and things are better. It is the therapist's job to make sure that perceived futures are possible. In some instances, a client may say something like, "If a miracle happened, then I wouldn't have been abused to begin with." The therapist must acknowledge that this is what the client would like, but also that some things are unchangeable. Focus is on what is possible and changeable. Even if the person says that the miracle would involve a change in someone else or a change in feelings, the therapist can follow up with a question about things within the client's control and influence. The therapist might respond, "Well, if somehow the miracle erased your abuse, what kinds of things would you be doing tomorrow after you wake up?" The focus on *actions* moves the discussion into the realm in which the person has some choices and power to make changes.

The Crystal Ball

Erickson (1954) would often use the image of crystal balls to help his patients to create change in their lives. In the waking state, he would ask his patient to state all that he or she wanted to have change in the future. He would then induce trance, and have the patient hallucinate a series of crystal balls. Each one would depict the patient in situations at different times in life. Peering into the crystal ball that symbolized the future, Erickson would suggest that the patient could envision how to achieve a preferred outcome (a time when the patient's problem was no longer a problem). He would also inquire about what had happened in the psychotherapy that helped the patient to move on. After the person had given a detailed description of both the process of solving the problem and the outcome, Erickson would suggest amnesia for the hallucination; the patient would be directed to forget about the future they had described in which things had worked out.

Once the client was again in the waking state, Erickson would suggest that he or she do the things envisioned while in trance to achieve the desired future. Many of Erickson's patients would go out and do what they had described in trance. He was somehow helping his patients to develop a blueprint for their future actions. This future-oriented work would impact the patients' actions in the present—which would, in turn, affect their futures.

Most of us have the idea that the past or present determines the present and the future. What if the future determined the present? If you knew that you were going to win the lottery tomorrow, would you be reading this book? Some of you would, but more than likely, most of you wouldn't! Or more, poignantly, if you knew someone you loved dearly was going to die in the next hour, would you be reading this? People's expectations of what the future will hold have an unmistakable effect on their present actions.

Videotape Descriptions

When assisting clients in creating futures with possibilities, it can be helpful to have them describe a time down the road when things are going the way they like. As previously discussed, one way to do this is to have the client give a video description (Hudson & O'Hanlon, 1991; O'Hanlon & Wilk, 1987) of the future:

> Let's say that a few weeks or months of time had elapsed and your problem had been resolved. If you and I were to watch a videotape of your life in the future, what would you be doing on that tape that would show that things were better?

Videotape descriptions can provide a picture of what clients will be doing in terms of action when they are no longer being oppressed by the aftereffects of sexual abuse. The therapist can then begin to help the client move toward those preferred realities.

These three approaches can help clients to rehabilitate or create a vision of a future with possibilities. We can then work backward from the future to the present, to figure out what they could do currently, if indeed, that were their future.

People who come to therapy do have some sense, however small, of the future. Otherwise, why would they bother with therapy? But they may show up in your office and say something on the order of, "I don't have a future" or "I don't have any possibilities." Woe to you if you believe they have no possibilities. Our friend and colleague Steve Gilligan says that clients sometimes come to therapy and attempt to hypnotize therapists with the idea that they *are* what they're experiencing. Either verbally or nonverbally, it's as if they are saying, "I'm depression. When you look at me, you will only see depression, not me. Go deeply into the depression trance. You will see nothing but depression when you look at me. Go deeply." They will give you the message that there are no possibilities. It is important to avoid being inducted into that vision and to help clients discover a vision of themselves where things work out.

SIGNPOSTS TO PREFERRED FUTURES

If you were to take a cross-country trip, it's likely that you would first determine where you wanted to go. If you were heading to a familiar place, you would probably know how to get there without having to be concerned with a map. You could simply look for those highway signs, mile markers, or landmarks that had previously guided you to your destination. Similarly, when clients who are suffering the aftereffects of sexual abuse are clearer about where they want to go, therapists can help them identify signs that they are moving in the direction of their preferred futures.

FUTURE PULL: CREATING OR EVOKING
A COMPELLING FUTURE

Finding a Vision for the Future

As in Viktor Frankl's story, having a vision for the future can be of great help in surviving trauma and in taking steps to create a better present and preferred future. The following questions might help your clients and you clarify their visions for the future and their life purpose:

- ❖ What is your life purpose?

- ❖ What is your vision of your preferred future?

- ❖ What dreams did you or do you have for your life?

- ❖ What are you here on the planet for?

- ❖ What are human beings on the planet for, in your view?

- ❖ What area do you think you could make a contribution in?

- ❖ What kinds of things compel you?

- ❖ What makes your heart sing?

Dealing with and Dissolving Barriers to the Preferred Future

Sometimes people know what they would like to do with their lives or what future they would like to have happen, but they cannot get there because they perceive insurmountable barriers in their way. They have fears of success or fears of failure. They think they are inadequate to the task of making the dream happen, or they think certain things must happen before they begin to pursue their dreams. These questions might help identify and surmount these barriers:

❖ What, in your view, stops you from realizing your visions or getting to your goals?

❖ What are you afraid of?

❖ What do you believe must happen before you can realize your visions and goals?

❖ What are the actions you haven't taken to make your dreams and visions come true?

❖ What are the real-world barriers you must deal with to realize your dreams and visions?

❖ What would your models, mentors, or people you admire do if they were you to realize this dream or vision?

❖ What are you not doing, feeling, or thinking that they would in this situation?

❖ What are you doing, feeling, or thinking that they wouldn't?

Making an Action Plan to Reach the Preferred Future

Having a vision of the future and even realizing what fears and perceived barriers stand in its way are helpful steps—but that clarity doesn't guarantee that that future will be achieved. A plan of action is also necessary. Viktor Frankl could not just imagine better days. He had to get up and walk that day in the snowy field. Then, when he finally emerged from the death camp, he had to begin to write books and give lectures. The following questions can help people begin to formulate and put into practice actions that will likely create their preferred futures:

- ❖ What could you do in the near future that would be steps toward realizing your visions and dreams?

- ❖ What would you do as soon as you leave here?

- ❖ What would you do tonight?

- ❖ What feeling would you have in your body as you took those steps?

- ❖ What would you be thinking that would help you take those steps?

- ❖ What images or metaphors are helpful to you in taking these steps?

For most abused people who seek therapy, just turning their gaze from the past to the future is a major reorientation. This reorientation can provide information about directions for treatment, shed light on the purpose for the client's life, and instill or restore hope. But we don't ignore the past. In Chapter Five, we show how the therapist can orient to the past in a way that helps the client move on, rather than repeat the trauma or dwell there.

SUMMARY POINTS
CHAPTER FOUR

❖ People who have been traumatized often have a sense that the future will be a repetition of the traumatic past or worse.

❖ This method of getting people moving involves helping them discover, create, or rehabilitate a sense of a future that will be different and better than the past.

❖ We offer several language methods for creating or restoring a sense of possibilities. We get people to orient to their preferred futures by:

1. Getting them to imagine that a miracle has occurred in which their problems have been resolved.

2. Having them imagine they can see it in a crystal ball.

3. Getting them to describe it as if it were being shown on a videotape.

❖ Sometimes it's not enough to get people to imagine a preferred future: You have to help them both make an action plan and deal with perceived or actual barriers to achieving that future.

CHAPTER
FIVE

The Web of Relationship

ACKNOWLEDGING THE FACT
AND EXPERIENCE OF
SEXUAL ABUSE

MARILYN VANDERBURR, A FORMER Miss America, was sexually abused when she was young. For years following the abuse, she suffered terrible aftereffects. One day, she was riding in the first-class section of a plane and became involved in a conversation with the man seated next to her. He told her all about his work and what he did, and then politely inquired as to what she did. She told him that he probably didn't want to know what she did. But he assured her that he did want to know. She then told him that she was horribly sexually abused throughout her childhood by her father. It had taken her years to come to terms with the abuse, and to recognize the effects that it had on her life and to begin to speak about it. Now her life's work and mission had become one of educating other people about sexual abuse. She told the man that she wanted to help others to heal and prevent further child sexual abuse. This was a pretty heavy topic for her fellow traveler, so he began to turn away in embarrassment. But she stopped him. She put her hand on his arm and said, "And now I'll tell you how to respond to me now that I've told you that." He numbly nodded. She said, "I'd like you to look me in the eye and say, 'I'm terribly sorry that happened to you.'" The man followed her instructions and replied, "I'm terribly sorry that happened to you."

This is an important story, in part because Ms. vanderBurr knew that telling her story was part of her healing. She was also wise enough (probably a wisdom gained through painful experience) to know what she needed to hear right after she had told her story to avoid feeling shamed or invalidated at that vulnerable moment.

So there are two points we'd like to make in this chapter. One is that because we don't encourage people to relive their abuse or dwell on the past in our treatment, it doesn't mean we don't deal with the past at all. We do. We allow and at times encourage people to tell the truth or their story about their abuse, which can be very healing for some. The second point is that there is a crucial difference between speaking about one's abuse and reliving or reexperiencing it. The latter is generally fraught with danger and is unnecessary. There are ways to encourage and support people who are dealing with the past without inviting them to be retraumatized by reliving the abuse.

Some years ago, Bill came across two different studies in separate journals (unfortunately lost to memory at this point) that reported opposite data regarding Holocaust survivors. One had found that those survivors who never talked about their experiences were better adjusted in their current lives. It was as if they had sealed away those horrifying incidents in the past. The other study had found that those survivors who continued to talk about the Holocaust and speak of their experiences had the lowest levels of depression. Perhaps these two studies were measuring different things and that is why they arrived at such disparate conclusions. But our view is that it illustrates well that each person has his or her own way to successfully deal with trauma. Novelist Robert B. Parker (1995) wrote in *Thin Air*:

> Some people . . . even some very intelligent people, even now and then some very intelligent shrinks, sometimes think that not talking about things is a handicap. For the people who aren't talking about things, however, it is a way to control feelings so you won't be tripping over them while you're trying to do something useful. Containment is not

limitation. It is an alternative to being controlled by your feelings. (p. 107)

Our respectful approach does not say, "You must remember and deal with your past. It's the only way to heal," or just as oppressively, "There's no need to revisit your past. It's dead and gone. You only have the present and future." For some people, it is crucial to speak about their experiences of abuse, and the retelling becomes part of their healing. There seems to be something about speaking to others about traumatic experiences that can counteract the shame one feels or that sheds light on something that might fester if kept in the secret dark inside.

In this chapter, then, we show some ways of inviting this truth-telling without having the person have to relive and reexperience the terrible trauma from which they have already suffered too much. Or as Kenneth Auchincloss has said, "It is one thing to learn about the past; it is another to wallow in it."

SOLUTION-FOCUSED RECOVERY SCALE

Yvonne Dolan has developed a scale (see Table 5.1) for clients who are suffering the aftereffects of sexual abuse. The scale can be used in a number of contexts. This form, which is generally filled out at the beginning or near the beginning of treatment, has several useful features. First, it helps to normalize clients' experiences. Second, it focuses on abilities, not inabilities; the categories are all stated in the positive, not the negative. Lastly, and of importance in this discussion, it acknowledges the current experience of clients related to their abuse. People are able to use this

TABLE 5.1
SOLUTION-FOCUSED RECOVERY SCALE
FOR SURVIVORS OF SEXUAL ABUSE

Name _____ Date _____

Please answer all questions beside each item below, indicate the degree
to which it occurs.

	Not at All	Just a Little	Pretty Much	Very Much
Able to think/talk about trauma				
Able to think/talk about things other than the trauma				
Sleeps OK				
Feels part of the family				
Stands up for self				
Maintains physical appearance (nails, hair, etc.)				
Goes to work				
Engages in social activities outside home				
Able to leave the house				
Cares for child, loved ones				
Cares for pets, plants				
Goes out for dinner				
Shows healthy appetite				
Adapts to new situations				
Telephones friends and loved ones				
Laughs at something funny				
Able to look loved ones, friends in the eye				
Able to look strangers in the eye				
Able to shake hands				
Holds hands with loved one				
Kisses loved one on the cheek				
Kisses husband/wife or boyfriend/girlfriend on the mouth				

TABLE 5.1 (Continued)				
	Not at All	Just a Little	Pretty Much	Very Much
Enjoys lovemaking				
Initiates lovemaking				
Bathes normally				
Interested in the future				
Pursues leisure activity				
Engages in new recreational activity/new interest				
Takes protective measures inside and outside the house				
Able to discriminate between supportive and nonsupportive relationships				
Chooses supportive relationships				
Initiates conversation with family, friends, or coworkers				
Able to initiate conversations with acquaintances and strangers				
Able to relax without drugs or alcohol				
Tolerates criticism well				
Accepts praise well				
Other signs of recovery				
Comments				

focus to recount the ways they are affected by the after-effects of the abuse.

The Recovery Scale also provides a measurement for change. By having clients fill out the form again at differing times during treatment, the therapist can get an idea of how things have changed or are changing. Sometimes, clients have difficulty recognizing change, and this form can help identify movement in specific areas, which may be difficult for clients and therapist to see.

INDIVIDUAL VERSUS PUBLIC OR GROUP DISCLOSURE

We have found there is a difference in the effect of a person telling his or her truth in a group setting than in an individual context. The group setting has a de-shaming effect that seems to decrease the need to retell the story. In the more private setting of one-to-one therapy, there seems to be less de-shaming and more invitation to dwell on or repeat the story again and again. It may be that the individual setting more closely resembles the secrecy of the original shameful abuse situation.

We do not tell people not to tell their story when in individual treatment, but we do not usually pursue or encourage the telling in that setting. When it seems appropriate, we recommend the group context for that.

GOING PUBLIC: A TIME-LIMITED GROUP PROCESS

Public witnessing seems to be a powerful thing as people are able to take a stand against shame. In individual therapy it is more difficult to replicate this process because clients expect their therapists to understand and accept them.

In this section, we outline a five-session, time-limited group process that can help people to move on when they are stuck in the healing process. As mentioned, speaking in a more public or social forum may decrease or eliminate feelings of shame related to the abuse. When in a group, others are around speaking the same kind of truth, which can produce a powerful normalizing and de-shaming effect. Each group member hears others speak about their abuse. Although some features are particular to each person's experience, members often recognize shared features. A positive effect of this shared experience stems from the participants' experiences being acknowledged as valid or "normal." For this and other reasons, we find that these time-limited group experiences can have a multiplied effect compared with individual work.

Why time-limited? Because we are making a distinction between treatment and recovery. As with chemical dependency, treatment can be short, time-limited, and very focused on stopping the problematic or symptomatic behavior and initiating the recovery process. Conversely, recovery may take years, or even a lifetime. In the group, our purpose is to do treatment. Thus, our group model is designed to help people to become unstuck and move on—not to resolve every possible issue that surfaces.

We limit group treatment to five sessions (typically, meetings are held one day a week for two hours over five consecutive weeks). We have found that groups work best with 8 to 10 participants.

Session 1

During the initial session, the purpose of the group is discussed first. We explain that we emphasize helping people to become unstuck and move on, not on resolving every issue.

Following this opening explanation, the participants introduce themselves. Then all the group members are asked to imagine a future in which they have resolved the abuse and it no longer haunts them. What kinds of things would they be doing, thinking, feeling, and experiencing that they don't typically have in their lives currently? How would other people know that they had resolved these issues or reached that future? What would be the first sign that they are moving in that direction (it may have happened already since they signed up for the group).

The group leader then has each person rate where he or she is on a scale of 1 to 100 with respect to that future. For example, if a person says she is at a 65, the leader might ask where she would be when it was resolved. Would she be at a 75? An 80? Each week, the Future Scale can be used to measure change, and to inquire how that change has come about. The Future Scale can also be useful in determining whether something in the group has been unhelpful if the number has decreased.

We also ask participants what the first sign might be that they are moving in the direction of their vision or preferred future. The participants are then given a copy of the Solution-Focused Recovery Scale (Table 5.1). We ask each participant to fill out the Recovery Scale before the next session.

Next, Bill typically tells a story about his abuse by a grandfather. He almost never tells his story in individual therapy, as it may seem intrusive. In a group setting, it appears to have a different effect. It helps equalize the field (this is not some objectively distant therapist gazing at his subjects under the microscope) and open up the participants to taking the risk to speak about their abuse.

Next, each participant in turn, is asked one question about some aspect of his or her abuse (see Table 5.2). Group members can pass (not answer); say they don't know or aren't sure; say they aren't willing to answer; or they can answer. Hearing each person answer the questions normalizes and gives permission for many different experiences and for recognizing the similarities of experience. When the participants hear each other describe their experiences, they realize that they are not alone. And the process of getting each person's story one piece at a time helps the person to avoid collapsing into reliving the abuse experiences and regressing. It's not so overwhelming for the client.

In presenting the list of questions in Table 5.2, we want to stress to readers that the people in our groups have all previously decided that they were abused. Some of them have never spoken about it in public, but most of them have. Later in the chapter, we discuss the importance of not leading clients in the direction of "remembering," as it is easy to cloud or create memories. Used in another context, these questions could be very leading.

After each participant has answered the questions (and said anything else they want to say), we tell the Marilyn vander-Burr story described at the beginning of this chapter. Each member is then asked to teach the group and the leader what they need to hear or to do after having just publicly acknowledged their abuse. Sometimes people will ask for things that can be done or said within the group.

At the end of this first session, a short, 5- to 10-minute *healing trance* is done. The term healing trance comes from one of Bill's clients who had previously experienced hypnosis done in a regressive, information-gathering way. The hypnotherapist would lead this client back to her traumatic events and have her reexperience and report on her traumas during

---

TABLE 5.2
FACTUAL QUESTIONS ABOUT SEXUAL ABUSE

- How old were you when you were first sexually abused? How old were you when the sexual abuse stopped (if it ever has)?

- How long did the sexual abuse last?

- How or why did the sexual abuse stop?

- Who did you tell about the sexual abuse (if anyone) at the time?

- How did they respond when you had told them?

- Did they do anything to help or protect you or stop the sexual abuse?

- How many times (approximately) were you sexually abused?

- Were you abused by a member of your immediate family of origin (parent(s), stepparent(s), brother(s), sister(s))?

- Were you abused by a member of your extended family (aunt(s), uncle(s), grandparent(s), stepgrandparent(s), cousin(s))?

- Were you abused by a friend of the family or person whom your family trusted?

- Did the person or people who abused you touch your breasts/chest during the abuse?

- Did the person or people who abused you touch your vagina during the abuse?

- Did the person or people who abused you touch your penis during the abuse?

- Did the person or people who abused you touch your clitoris during the abuse?

- Did the person or people who abused you touch your anus during the abuse?

TABLE 5.2 (Continued)

- Did the person or people who abused you put his/her fingers inside your vagina during the abuse?

- Did the person or people who abused you put his penis inside your vagina during the abuse?

- Did the person or people who abused you put his/her fingers inside your anus during the abuse?

- Did the person or people who abused you put his penis inside your anus during the abuse?

- Did the person or people who abused you put his penis inside your mouth during the abuse?

- Did the person or people who abused you have you touch his penis (or her vagina) during the abuse?

- Did the person or people who abused you masterbate in front of you during the abuse?

- Did the person or people who abused you have you masterbate in front of him/her/them during the abuse?

- Did the person or people who abused you put anything besides parts of their body inside your anus/vagina or mouth during the abuse?

- Did the person or people who abused you tell you not to tell anyone about the abuse?

- What did they say would happen if you told about the abuse?

- Did the person or people who abused you threaten you if you told?

- Did the person or people who abused you say anything to you during the abuse? What?

- Whom have you ever told about the abuse?

- How did the people or person you told about the abuse respond?

trance. She found this both harrowing and exhausting. When she came to see Bill, he began doing a different kind of trance with her that was not directed toward remembering the past, but rather toward valuing herself in the present. She called these "healing trances," because she emerged from them energized and calm.

Group participants can join the healing trance or just watch it, depending on what is most comfortable and right for them. If they participate, they may choose to keep their eyes open or close them. This first group trance has to be somewhat general because only a certain amount of information has been shared so far. Later trances may be more detailed as the leader learns more about each participant. Here's an example of a brief healing trance:

> What I'd like to do is invite you, if you want and if it's right for you at this time, to go inside or focus your attention wherever you want to. To allow the possibility to experience a bit of what I call healing trance. Because what's available in this healing trance is for you to be validated where you are now, meaning that you can be distracted or you don't have to focus at this particular moment. You can think that this won't work for you or you can be afraid that it will work for you, and that you'll go deeply into trance. Anything about where you are, as much as possible, find out if you can make space or room for it, even if it seems like a distraction or you're not doing it right. What I'm going to do is invite you to a place that I think already exists inside you. A place where whatever is going on with you is valid and okay. A place that's so deeply inside you that it's beyond or beneath the evaluation that someone gave you about yourself or that you've made about yourself. Beyond the shame, beyond the invalidation that's been piled on top of it for years. Beyond the intrusions and injunctions of other people. A place where you're just okay as you are. A place where you don't need to

fix or change anything about yourself. A place where you can get behind the ideas of your badness or your shame. Get underneath those ideas and be able to take a look at those ideas, rather than be dominated by them. A place where you can actually experience your value. A place where you can experience the validation for where you are now. Especially if you don't think that you should be feeling or experiencing or thinking or imagining or responding as you are now. Whatever you're experiencing is okay even if you don't think it's okay, that's okay. Now, you may have varying reactions to that. You may be angry. You may be sad. You may be happy. You may feel okay about that. And you're invited to include your reactions to that, because I can't know everything about you. I just have a general idea. I think you're of value. You may disagree with that, but I think something inside you agrees with that. And also something inside you, I believe, has a vision of the future, and a mission for why you're here on this particular planet at this particular time. Something you have to contribute, even if you doubt your contribution or your ability to contribute. Something you have to give to other people and to receive from other people. And I really don't know if you know about that or are in touch with it or if you believe that. I just want to invite that possibility. And it's an invitation with an RSVP, from your own experience. So you can respond as much or as little to this as is right for you. You can use these words to heal and to reconnect, or you can let any of the words that I say that haven't really fit for you, have invalidated you, or aren't right for you, just go by the wayside. You can leave them to the side or transform them into something that really makes sense to you. And now at your own rate and your own pace, you can begin to reorient to the present time and the present place. If there's something happening inside that you want to continue, you can begin to bring closure to that in a way that's right for you. And if you had your eyes closed, you can open them when you're ready, and continue to orient to the present time and the present place.

During this part of the group, some participants will look around the whole time, and some people will really get into the experience. Many people find the brief trance the most meaningful part of the group. Other people find it irrelevant. The hypnotic experience brings the first session to a close.

Session 2

The second meeting begins by focusing on change. The leader asks about any change that has happened between Sessions 1 and 2. Using the Future Scale question again, the therapist asks, "In terms of the Scale, where are you now and what made a difference between the weeks?" Sessions 2 through 5 also include a brief (5- to 10-minute) lecture. The lecture in Session 2 is about *dissociated, devalued,* and *disowned* aspects of self. The participants learn that the dissociated components usually show up in one of two ways, as either inhibited/diminished experience or intrusive experience. A discussion takes place during this minilecture in which each person has the opportunity to talk about any aspects of self that he or she may have dissociated, devalued, or disowned. These aspects must be tied to what is troubling the group member in the present.

The "now focus" is a crucial part of the group process because it keeps things focused on what people are complaining about. When it is clear what aspects of self might have split off or been devalued, each person makes a plan for taking one step toward valuing the devalued aspect (see the worksheet in Table 5.3). Session 2 of the group ends with another brief healing trance.

TABLE 5.3
WORKSHEET FOR DEVELOPING A RELATIONSHIP
WITH DEVALUED/DISOWNED/DISSOCIATED ASPECTS OF SELF

1. Identify any aspects of yourself or your experience that you have found difficult to tolerate or have avoided or inhibited. If you don't really have a clue, this is some part of your life in which your experience is intruded on (like flashbacks) or in which you are inhibited or numb (as in you never get angry or you go numb when you start to have sex). This might involve parts of your body (e.g., your genitals, your face), your body in general (e.g., you have found it difficult to look at your body in the mirror, you always dress in the closed out of sight), your relationships with other people (e.g., rejection or conflict), your feelings (e.g., anger is not okay, sadness is intolerable), your sensations (e.g., sexual feelings, tickling), or perceptions (smells really get to you, you are haunted by images of the abuse).

(continued)

TABLE 5.3 (Continued)
2. Plan one thing you could do to start to approach and value that aspect of your experience rather than avoid or inhibit it.

TABLE 5.3 (Continued)
3. Imagine yourself feeling or experiencing that aspect of your experience in the presence of someone who cares for you unconditionally.

(continued)

TABLE 5.3 (Continued)

4. List and challenge any blaming, impossibility, self-devaluing, or nonchoice beliefs your problem is trying to convince you of.

Session 3

The group again begins with a discussion about what changes or results occurred during or after the prior group session. Next, group members again rate themselves on the Future Scale. The focus remains on the differences that people are experiencing.

The topic for this session is *patterns.* That is, how people get into that same damn thing over and over again, and how they can make little changes to interrupt or stop the pattern. Each person is asked to come up with one thing to break up the problematic pattern he or she is experiencing. It could be something like changing one word that the person uses. For example, if someone's pattern is to repeat over and over again, "I'm bad," then he or she might add a word and say, "I think I'm bad." A slight change in the pattern is all that is necessary. It could be a change in a pattern of speaking, action, interaction, body behavior, or whatever realm the client is experiencing being stuck. Participants are given a handout on changing patterns (see Table 5.4). The third session also ends with a healing trance.

Session 4

The change experienced by the participants is again discussed, and the Future Scale question of 1 to 100 is asked. The minilecture topic of this fourth session is *boundaries.* Again a handout is provided (see Table 5.5). Two variations of boundaries are discussed. The first is when a person doesn't have sufficient boundaries and people intrude. The other is when they have too many boundaries and the person is isolated. When people don't have good boundaries, it's like a castle with big walls, no doors, and a moat. The person stuck inside the walls of the castle can't be reached

TABLE 5.4 CHANGING PATTERNS
Identifying Problem Patterns

- Identify problem patterns by noticing actions that are repetitive, what people in several settings (home, work) complain about, and/or a similar label that others give the person in various settings.

- Remember to focus on the doing of the problem, not being the problem or the feeling associated with the problem. (A person can feel shy but does not have to *do* shy.) Use videotalk to describe how clients do the problem. How do they *do* anger, jealousy, shyness, or borderline? Recognize triggers (invitations) to the patterns. What are the typical steps leading up to the problem?

- With interpersonal patterns, either person can change the problem pattern—it's hard to do a tango when the other person starts doing the fox trot. Remind clients that the ability to change a problem pattern does not mean that they are to blame for the creation of that pattern or problem.

Changing Problem Patterns

- When they would usually do the pattern, get the person or the couple/family members/friends to do anything different from their old patterns that is legal, ethical, and not harmful:

  Change actions (sequence, antecedents, consequences, repetitive/invariant actions and interactions, body behavior).

  Change location/setting.

  Change timing (frequency, time of occurrence, duration).

  Use humor.

  Change the nonverbals (voice tones, gestures, body movements, eye contact, etc.) around the pattern.

TABLE 5.4 (Continued)
• Search for exceptions. What is the person or others around him or her doing when the problem doesn't happen? Identify the solution or exception patterns and get the person to do more of those patterns in place of those that don't work.
• Search in another setting for patterns that work better (at work, with friends, in other family relationships, with hobbies). Borrow the skills and creativity they use in those other settings and apply them to changing the pattern.
Remember what Rita Mae Brown and some 12-steppers say: "Insanity is doing the same thing over and over again and expecting different results."

and thus can't be hurt, but that person can't be nurtured either. Conversely, if the castle is not built up and always has its drawbridge down with people coming and going, then that person has poor boundaries. Some people vacillate between these extremes. Others experience both at the same time.

There are many ways of negotiating the space in between diffuse and rigid boundaries. Here are two possibilities. Through either a hypnotic or nonhypnotic experience, suggest that the participants each make a castle with a drawbridge that they can open or close. They can decide whom to let in and when they are to leave. Another possibility would be to use a doorknob metaphor. Instead of having the doorknob on the outside where anyone can come in and intrude, the person can have it on the inside. That way they can lock the door when they want, and unlock it when they want.

TABLE 5.5
RECOGNIZING AND STANDING FOR YOUR BOUNDARIES

Boundaries around Self

- Letting others touch you/various parts of your body.
- Letting others tell you what you think/fell/experience.
- Letting others communicate with you (talking/writing/contacting/visiting/phoning).
- Providing access to home (keys, visits, phone calls, warnings).
- Giving money to others/accepting money from others.
- Touching others/various parts of their bodies (with or without permission).
- Telling others what you think/fell/experience.

Boundaries around Relationships

- Setting limits for the other person's behavior when the person is with you and when not with you.
- Keeping your word and holding others to their word.

Hints

- Where/with whom have you not put up boundaries/limits when it would have served you well to do so?
- Where/with whom have you not let people, feelings in when it would have served you well to do so?
- You have the right to set boundaries, to say no and say yes.
- Get clear on your boundaries/limits.
- Stand for your boundaries/limits.
- Ask for respect of boundaries/limits from those with whom you interact.
- If the boundaries/limits have been violated, get/give a clear statement of accountability, an apology (if appropriate), and a reestablishment of the commitment to the boundary. Arrange for restitution/amends if necessary.

These doorknobs also allow the person to invite people in or have them leave whenever they wish.

After the lecture about boundaries, group members are asked to describe how these metaphors fit their lives. Each person is then asked to make a plan for doing one thing to change their boundary patterns in the next week.

Near the end, the participants are given a copy of the Solution-Focused Recovery Scale and asked to fill it out and bring it back for the final session. As with the previous groups, a healing trance closes out the session.

Session 5

After discussing the changes that have occurred from the last session and in between the meetings, the members are asked to rate themselves on the 1 to 100 Future Scale. In addition, each participant goes over the highlights of the Solution-Focused Recovery Scale and how it has changed since the group started.

The minilecture is about *rituals* including connection/ stability and transition rituals (discussed in Chapter Seven). Each person is asked to plan a healing, connective, or transition ritual and given a handout to assist in designing and carrying out the ritual (see Table 5.6). Following this, the participants speak about the changes they have made. They are also given the chance to communicate any messages they want to one another to close out the group.

A longer healing trance is done at the end of this, the final group session. As the group ends, the participants are asked to write the leader in a month. They're asked to describe what changes they have made since the group ended, what else has happened with them, and what ideas they may have that could make the group better for future participants.

TABLE 5.6
SYMBOLS AND HEALING RITUALS

Find a Symbolic Object

- Find or create a physical object that is associated with or represents the trauma, person, or feeling. This can be done by determining what representative object you possess, can buy, or can get or by writing, drawing, or sculpting. You may prefer using a resource symbol. That is, rather than finding a symbol for the trauma or problem, you can find a solution symbol, something that represents safety, good feelings, and so on.

Create a Healing Transition Ritual*

- Clarify what the purpose of the ritual is and what is still unfinished for you.

- Prepare for the ritual by deciding what symbols you will use, when you will do the ritual, who else will be included, what you will wear, where you will perform the ritual, and what you need to do to get ready emotionally and psychologically to do the ritual. You might want to fast or write before doing the ritual.

- Do the ritual.

- Find a way to make a transition from the ritual back into your everyday life. Take a bath, go for a short or long trip, go for a walk, write, fast, meditate, and so on.

- If it is appropriate, arrange for friends, significant others, or family members to attend a celebration of the completion of the ritual and your determination to move on.

* The word ritual has negative associations for some people. "Ceremony" or "healing task" might be better terms for those people.

TABLE 5.6 (Continued)

Create Healing Connective Rituals

- Recall some regular habit or activity from the time before the trauma or disruption that helped connect you to yourself or to others. If you cannot recall any or the ones you recall are not appropriate, create a habit or an activity for connection.

- Make a regular (daily, weekly, seasonally, yearly, etc.) habit of doing the activity. You may need to schedule it until to becomes habitual.

THIS MODEL AVOIDS THE PROBLEMS OF LEADING AND FALSE MEMORY

Since this chapter focuses on truth-telling and healing trances, it is appropriate to speak to one of the controversial issues in the field, "false memories." How can therapists determine whether clients are telling them the truth about childhood sexual abuse? Frankly, we can't. Therapists have different roles from lawyers, judges, or forensic investigators. We don't deal so directly with the external reality that people live, except when we see people conjointly, in couples or family therapy, or in residential or inpatient treatment, in which case we still have but a small slice of their lives available for observation.

There is a popular saying among some child sexual abuse experts: "Believe the children!" In our experience, children do not always tell the truth (about sexual abuse or other matters), but in most cases it is best to err on the side of caution in protecting the child. Finding physical evidence and witnesses are important. But in the absence of these, with compelling enough testimony from the child that seems un-coerced, it is generally best to ensure that the person who has been accused of perpetrating abuse does not have un-supervised access to the child until the matter is settled. There are some circumstances, however, that should make one more skeptical about the accusation:

❖ When a child claims or children claim repeated, group abuse and no physical evidence or witnesses outside the child or children can be found.

❖ When the child had no recollection or report of abuse until repeatedly or persistently questioned by a ther-apist.

❖ There is a custody battle or bitter divorce going on and there was no evidence or accusation of abuse before the battle started.

Adults' memories of childhood abuse require a different approach. With them, it's best to err on the side of caution in going public with the accusation, confronting the alleged abuser(s) with the accusation, and cutting off contact with the alleged abuser(s) or the family. Although the issue is not yet scientifically settled, there is evidence that memory is not always accurate (like a tape recorder) and can be dis-torted by input, coding, or recall errors. Memory can also be influenced by current contexts and beliefs, and direct and indirect suggestions.

Some therapists see constellations of symptoms that lead them to conclude, and sometimes definitively tell clients, that clients who show these symptoms have been abused. Allega-tions or memories of sexual abuse cannot be conclusively proven by the presence of symptoms without corroborating physical evidence or direct witnesses. In our experience, most people who have been traumatized do remember the trauma.

In this model, we bypass the whole issue of leading people toward remembering things falsely because we don't encourage them to go back to the past. If they revisit the past on their own, we will do what we usually do—acknowledge their experience and invite them into new possibilities.

With some traditional models of treating abuse, the therapist leads the client in the direction he or she feels is correct or most therapeutic (usually that means remembering and reliving the abuse). The theory of the therapist dictates the direction of the treatment. We don't hold the preconceived idea that we know what is right for our clients, whether in their lives after therapy or as to the right pathway to healing. We trust that our clients will find, often with our help, the best pathways to heal themselves. As discussed earlier, it is similar to the sport of curling. When a client heads in a particular direction, we sweep open possibilities and then pay attention to the path they take and which possibilities speak to them. We do not direct the client unless there is a risk of harm to self or others (in which case, any therapist must take action to ensure the safety of the client):

Bob attended Bill's supervision group, where a female client came in for a session. The woman had been involved with a psychiatrist who had used hypnosis with her on a regular basis. Since she had remained stuck in her experience, she came to see Bill. During the trancework, the woman came to a bridge. She had encountered this bridge before, and her reaction was that she became upset.

Bill asked, "What's happening?"

She replied, "I don't want to go over the bridge. I'm scared."

"You don't have to go over the bridge if that's not right for you. What do you feel like you need to do?" asked Bill.

She responded, "I don't know. I'm scared."

Bill answered, "It's okay to be scared, and you don't have to cross the bridge."

When the woman finished her trancework, she explained that in her previous hypnotic experiences with her former psychiatrist, he had told her that she had to cross the bridge and face her fears. She further remarked that he had dictated that she take other paths during trance that she did not want to follow. This was excruciatingly painful for her. The woman related that she appreciated that Bill had trusted her sense that she knew what she needed. It may be that she will cross the bridge at some point, and it's equally possible that she may never do it. However, should she choose to, it will be because she felt it was right for her, not because a therapist told her it was what she needed.

BEWARE OF THEORY COUNTERTRANSFERENCE OR WHERE DID ALL THESE MULTIPLE PERSONALITIES COME FROM?

We have touched on the idea that therapists' models of therapy can dominate the clients' experience in a sometimes intrusive and unhelpful way. Nowhere is this danger more apparent than in the treatment of multiple personality, or what is now called Dissociative Identity Disorder (American Psychiatric Association, 1994). For years, multiple personality disorder (MPD) was rarely diagnosed. True cases of MPD were often missed or misdiagnosed. Recently, the situation has reversed. MPD is now an epidemic (North, Ryall, Ricci, &

Wetzel, 1993). Colin Ross (1989), a well-known expert on MPD writes, "Within a span of ten years, we may evolve from extreme underdiagnosis of MPD to a situation in which the major problem is false positive diagnosis." Prior to 1944, a total of 76 cases of multiple personality disorder had been reported in the psychiatric literature (Taylor & Martin, 1944). Because they were so rare and dramatic, most cases were probably written up. By 1970, 14 more cases had been reported, 6 of which were by one clinician, making for a total of 90 cases, almost all of which were in North America (Aldridge-Morris, 1989). By 1986, it was estimated that 6,000 cases of MPD had been diagnosed in North America (Aldridge-Morris, 1989; Coons, 1986; Ross, 1989). In 1986, Frank Putnam wrote, "More cases of MPD have been reported within the last five years than in the preceding two centuries." In addition, the average number of personalities "discovered" has risen from 2 from 1840 until 1944 to 25 in 1990. The maximum number of personalities reported has risen from 3 in 1850 to over 300 in 1990 (and still rising) (North et al., 1993).

What is happening here? Perhaps there were cases of multiplicity that clinicians missed in previous decades. But 6,000 of them (now, it is surely many more than 6,000, but the number is hard to ascertain)? And since some cases were discovered and treated, how come those early pioneers did not discover 300 personalities in their cases? They used hypnosis and they clearly believed in the possibility of multiple personalities.

What is operating here, in our opinion, is "theory countertransference" (Hubble & O'Hanlon, 1992). This is our name for the phenomenon that happens when a therapist unwittingly imposes his or her theory on the client and becomes convinced that the data arose spontaneously from the client. We must be wary of two extremes: One is ignoring, denying, or minimizing the client's reports of multiplicity and abuse, and the other is imposing or leading the client in the direction of multiplicity and abuse "memories." Following their account of the treatment of multiple personality in their popular book, *The Three Faces of Eve*, authors Thigpen and Cleckley (1992) received a flood of inquiries and requests for treatment from people who had been diagnosed by their therapists or had self-diagnosed MPD. They found virtually no cases of true MPD among the cases referred to them. They wrote (1984) that MPD patients seem to have "a competition to see who can have the greatest number of alter personalities." (Unfortunately, there also appears to be a competition among some therapists to see who can have the greatest number of multiple personality cases.) (Thigpen, C. H., & Cleckley, H. M. (1992) Revised Ed. *The Three Faces of Eve*. Kingsport, TN: Kingsport Press.):

Bill had a client come to see him several years after having seen him for marital therapy. She reported that in the interim she had begun seeing a psychiatrist in town, who had used trance with her and discovered that she was multiple personality. Since Bill had seen no evidence of the multiplicity during her previous treatment and he knew that this psychiatrist was quite enamored with the "multiple personality" label of late, he expressed surprise and the gentlest of skepticisms. He said, "You know, I'm a bit surprised to hear that diagnosis, since I didn't see any evidence of it when I knew you before. I also know that Dr. M is hot on this diagnosis. Do you think this was really your experience or was it his idea that shaped your experience?" She assured Bill that it was her experience. But the next session, she told Bill she had been thinking of their conversation and had reconsidered. "I was always multiple," she said, "only it was in the back of my mind. His work made it come to the front of my mind and I became aware

that not everyone had different parts that were so indepen-
dent inside. But, you know, I think working with him has
made me too multiple." "Too multiple? How?" asked Bill.
"Well, before it was just these parts of myself inside. Nobody
else knew about them. But since I've worked with him, other
people can sometimes see the other personalities. They have
been taking over and talking, sometimes in a baby voice, to
my children and my husband. One time in a store, one of
them came out and the clerk looked at me rather strangely."
We jointly decided that it was important that her experience
of multiplicity was acknowledged in the therapy, but that it
was not so helpful to be encouraged to act out the multiplicity
in the world.

It is also important to ask clients if this view of themselves
as multiple is helpful. Our experience has been that sometimes it is and sometimes it isn't. In our view, there is no
such "thing" as a personality (i.e., it's not a measurable, ob-
servable entity); it is merely a construct of language. Pathol-
ogists have done a lot of autopsies and never discovered a
personality (or multiple personalities). Nevertheless, each of
the authors has a sense that he has a personality. So, to us,
personality is a story, not a truth, albeit a compelling story.
Still, being a story, there is some room for change. In the
next chapter, we discuss how to turn impossible, unhelpful
stories into more validating, hopeful stories.

SUMMARY POINTS
CHAPTER FIVE

❖ Even though we don't encourage people to regress and relive their abuse traumas, some people find it healing to tell their stories and speak their truth about their abuse.

❖ Our experience shows that this truth-telling is best done in a group setting because it can powerfully decrease shame and normalize more effectively.

❖ There is a way to help people tell their story without collapsing into reliving or reexperiencing it. Again, group settings are more conducive to this process, since each group member can tell a bit of his or her story at a time.

❖ Be careful about suggesting memories of abuse or cocreating multiple personality. Clients with boundary difficulties can be very susceptible to intrusions of other people's ideas. Because our model is permissive and present- to future-oriented and problem-driven, it can bypass the leading aspects of traditional, regressive, cathartic approaches.

CHAPTER
SIX

Weaving Possibility Stories

*B*ILL GOT THIS STORY *from a book he read as a teenager: Long ago, in Tibet, there was a ceremony held every 100 years, that Buddhist seekers could go through to attain enlightenment. In the ceremony, all the students would line up in their white robes. The lamas, the Tibetan priests, and the Dalai Lama, would line up before the students. The Dalai Lama would begin the ceremony, "This is the ceremony of The Room of 1,000 Demons. It is the ceremony for enlightenment and it only happens once every 100 years. You can only go through it now. If you choose not to, you will have to wait another 100 years. To help you make this decision, we'll tell you what The Room of 1,000 Demons ceremony is about.*

"In order to get into The Room of 1,000 Demons, you just open the door and walk in. The Room of 1,000 Demons is not very big. Once you enter, the door will close behind you. There is no doorknob on the inside of the door. In order to get out, you have to walk all the way through the room, find the doorknob (which is unlocked), open the door, and come out. That's all you have to do to be enlightened.

"But it's called The Room of 1,000 Demons because there are 1,000 demons in there. Those demons have the ability to take on the form of your worst fears. As soon as you walk in the room, those demons show you your worst fears. If you have a fear of heights, when you walk into the room it will appear as if you are standing on a narrow ledge of a tall building. If you have a fear of spiders, you'll be surrounded by the scariest eight-legged creatures imaginable. Whatever your fears are, the demons take those images from your mind and seem to make them real. In fact, they'll be so compellingly real, it will be very difficult to remember they're not.

"We can't come in and rescue you. That is part of the rules. If you go into The Room of 1,000 Demons, you have to make it out on your own. Some people never make it out the other side. They go into The Room of 1,000 Demons and become paralyzed with fright. And they stay trapped in The Room until they die. So, if you want to take the risk of entering The Room, that's fine. If you don't; if you want to go home, that's fine. You don't have to go through it. You can wait until you get incarnated again, come back in another 100 years, and try it again.

"If you want to go through, we have two hints for you. The first hint is, as soon as you go into The Room of 1,000 Demons, remember that what they show you isn't real. It's all from your own mind. Don't buy into it, it's an illusion. Of course, most of the people who went into the room before you couldn't remember that. It is very difficult to keep it in mind. The second hint has been more helpful for the people who made it out the other side and became enlightened. Once you go into the room, no matter what you see, no matter what you feel, no matter what you hear, no matter what you think, keep your feet moving. *If you keep your feet moving, you will eventually get to the other side, find the door, and come out."*

We view therapy as involving four domains: *experience, actions, views,* and *context.* As discussed in Chapters One and Two, all internal experience is okay. This includes feelings, inner sensations, fantasies, sensory perceptions, and sense of self. We strive to acknowledge, validate, and value clients' inner experience because this is who they are—their core sense of themselves.

But when we get to the realm of action, it is clear that some actions are okay and some are not. For example, a person might be cutting herself or yelling at strangers in stores. Thus, we encourage and try to promote actions that promote well-being, lead toward therapeutic goals, and are not harmful to self or others. Conversely, we discourage and oppose those actions that are unethical, lead away from or block established therapeutic goals, or are harmful to self or others. We have already detailed changing patterns of action in Chapter Three; in this chapter we focus on changing the views and the contexts surrounding the problem.

The views people have are twofold: One is what they are paying attention to in their lives and the other is the interpretations and meanings they add to the events and situations they face. The views that people have can be about the past, the present, the future, or their identities.

STORY-LAND: FOUR PROBLEMATIC STORIES

As with action, some views are okay and some are not. There are stories that validate, hold people accountable rather than blame them, and open up possibilities for change. There are also stories involving blame, invalidation, nonaccountability, and impossibility that we have found are troublesome for clients. We refer to these as the "Four Problematic Stories."

Stories of *blame* occur when a person is labeled (by themselves or someone else) as having bad intentions or bad personality traits. In the context of sexual abuse, this refers primarily to clients who self-blame or describe themselves as bad in some way. Clients who carry around these stories about themselves will often think things such as, "I'm bad because I was sexually abused" or "I must have wanted it." They either perceive themselves as damaged goods or attribute bad intentions to themselves.

Stories of *invalidation* are those that characterize clients as being abnormal or wrong in some way or give them the message that they can't trust their perceptions. Clients who are suffering the aftereffects of sexual abuse sometimes believe that they are crazy or that they can't do anything right. They may be further invalidated by others who say they are making it all up or are making too much of it and should just move on and forget about the past.

Nonaccountability stories involve people not accepting responsibility for themselves and their actions. At times, people will say things such as, "He made me do it," "I was drunk," or "I can't help it." People are accountable for the actions that they take (what they do with their bodies). This is very different from times when people have no choice and are intruded on without their consent. Then, the person(s) who committed the intrusive act(s) is accountable:

Bill had a client Kim, who had come in to work on the after-effects of the abuse she had suffered. When Kim first came in, she had the view that she was responsible for all the abuse. Kim thought she should have done something to stop it. After some discussion, it became apparent that under the circumstances, she hadn't really had a choice in the matter. Having realized that and done the other work she needed to do, Kim concluded therapy. A few years later, she returned and said she had something very important and difficult to discuss. Three times (out of the hundreds of times it had happened), she had sought out her abuser and made herself available for the abuse. Bill immediately tried to reassure her, telling Kim that she had been sexualized as a child and hadn't really been responsible. "No," the client told him firmly, "I know what you are trying to do and it won't work. Don't try to wave your therapeutic magic wand and free me from the responsibility on these incidents. I used to think I was responsible for it all, but now I'm telling you that it was just these three incidents. I was responsible for those. If you don't hold me responsible, then I can't hold him responsible for all those other times, since he was most probably abused himself. It's important that you hold me accountable." Bill quickly realized his mistake and began to help her come to terms with what she had done.

There are also stories of *impossibility.* These involve ideas that maintain that clients are unable to or are incapable of change. Clients who are suffering the aftereffects of sexual abuse often have the idea that nothing will ever change and there are no possibilities for them.

We want to challenge, create some doubt in, and stand against stories of blame, invalidation, nonaccountability, and those that close down possibilities. Meanwhile, we seek to amplify and nurture ideas that run counter to the four problematic stories. These are stories that:

- ❖ Allow for the possibility of change.

- ❖ Hold people accountable.

- ❖ Validate.

Table 6.1 gives the reader a map of the four major areas of intervention in this model for therapy with people who have been abused.

As Table 6.1 reflects, all experience is okay—the trick is to convey that to the client. First, it is important to acknowledge and validate clients' experience and sense of themselves as okay (if you don't do that, they probably won't be available to change). Then, when working on change, focus on the three other areas:

1. Changing the viewing.

2. Changing the doing.

3. Changing the context.

TABLE 6.1 FOUR AREAS FOR INTERVENTIONS IN THERAPY POLARITIES OF TROUBLESOME AFTEREFFECTS OF TRAUMA			
Experience	**Views**	**Actions**	**Context**
Feelings Sense of self Bodily sensations Sensory experience Automatic fantasies and thoughts	Points of view Attentional patterns Interpretations Explanations Evaluations Assumptions Beliefs Identity stories	Action patterns Interactional patterns Language patterns Nonverbal patterns	Time patterns Spatial patterns Cultural background and propensities Family/historial backgrond and propensities Biochemical/genetic background and propensities Gender training and propensities
Give messages of acceptance, validation, and acknowledgment. There is no need to change or analyze experience as it is not inherently a problem.	Challenge views that are: —Blaming — Support impossibility —Invalidating —Support nonaccountability or determinism. Offer new possibilities for attention.	Find patterns that are part of the problem and that are the "same damn thing over and over." Then suggest disrupting the problematic patterns or use solution patterns.	Suggest shifts in the context around the problem (e.g., changes in bio-chemistry, time, space, cultural habits and influences). Use these areas to normalize (and therefore value and validate) as well as to find the problem and solution patterns in any or all of the contextual factors.

We have used two methods to successfully change these areas. The first method is to find out what *hasn't* been working or is problematic in these areas and then to shift clients out of those unworkable patterns. The second method is to find out what works, has worked, or that clients would imagine would work in these areas, and encourage them to increase the workable patterns.

RECLAIMING AND REWRITING
IDENTITY STORIES

To fear is one thing. To let fear grab you by the tail and swing you around is another.

—Katherine Paterson

People develop certain ideas about who they are, based (in part) on messages they get from others around them and the culture they grow up in, and (in part) on the conclusions they make about themselves. The identity stories that people live by can either restrict or open up possibilities; they can validate or undermine. When people are suffering the aftereffects of sexual abuse, their identity stories or self-narratives often seem to be *problem saturated* (White & Epston, 1990). People who have been abused often live the stories of those who have intruded on them, instead of stories of their own choosing derived from their own sensibilities and voices. We seek to help clients rewrite their identity stories into ones that are less oppressive and undermining and more in keeping with their voices and preferences:

Jennifer, a client who saw Steffanie, Bill's wife, was troubled by the fact that she never really fought her father when he began to rape her as a child. She wriggled her hips, trying to get away, she said, but that only gave him the false message that she was getting turned on by what he did. When Steffanie did some work with Jennifer, she remembered that after her father had ejaculated in her, she had pushed him away. She hadn't remembered that part before. Jennifer smiled and laughed in relief after she remembered. "I did fight back!" She reported that she became more comfortable with sex with her husband after this memory. Jennifer also became more assertive and more confident in several areas of her life. When asked why, she replied, "I am a powerful woman!"

When people begin to think of themselves as the problem or as damaged, they begin to live in that problem-saturated story about themselves. We work to evoke alternative identity stories by highlighting aspects of people's current lives, their histories, and their inner views that don't fit with the unhelpful invalidating stories:

Phil, a young boy who had been sexually abused, molested several other children in the foster home in which he was living. When Phil was brought for counseling, he talked about how he got in trouble for "licking weenies." He knew that it was wrong, he said, but he just couldn't stop it. When asked about this, Phil said he would get this "bad" feeling and feel compelled to "lick weenies." When asked what he would call this "bad" influence, Phil decided it would be called "Death Breath." Phil was asked how he had come under Death Breath's influence and how he felt when he was under that influence. He replied that after he was abused by someone licking his weenie, he started to be visited by Death Breath. Phil felt bad when Death Breath visited him.

Next, Phil was asked how he would deal with a schoolmate who tried to get him in trouble by telling him to do bad things.

He said that he would tell the classmate that what he was suggesting was wrong and that he wouldn't do it. "Had he ever told Death Breath that Phil wouldn't go along with his plans?" No, he hadn't. "Could he?" Yes, he could. A plan was made that Phil would watch for Death Breath and catch him trying to get him to do bad things. Then he would practice standing up to this bully.

He had some success catching and standing up to Death Breath in the next few weeks. When he was asked what inside him helped him be strong enough to stand up to Death Breath, Phil said he thought it was his sadness. How did his sadness help him stand up to Death Breath? His sadness reminded him of how scared he had felt when someone had licked his weenie, and Phil didn't want to help Death Breath make another child so scared and sad. So, did that mean that he cared about other children and his caring joined with his sadness to help him be strong enough to stand up to Death Breath's bad influences? Yes, he replied.

THAT REMINDS ME OF A STORY:
METAPHORS FOR HEALING

For hundreds of years, stories have captivated people. Stories, fairy tales, myths, and metaphors are a universal means of communicating, and are an accepted part of nearly all walks of life. In many instances, stories shape our vision of the world in which we live. Although the degree to which they are used varies from society to society and culture to culture, the healing value of stories is widely recognized.

What is it about stories that makes them so healing? First, they engage people and hold their attention. Listeners wonder, "What's going to happen next?" and "How is it going to end?" When their attention is captured, it is more likely that they will receive the message or messages within the story. In addition to capturing attention, stories also allow people to create new meanings and understandings that can lead to possibilities. Stories are a way of accessing multiple pathways, all of which can help clients to unfreeze from the stuckness they are experiencing. Some of the ways that stories do this is by:

- ❖ Normalizing the experiences of clients.

- ❖ Acknowledging.

- ❖ Offering hope.

- ❖ Bypassing everyday conscious ways of processing information.

- ❖ Reminding clients of previous solutions and resources.

Stories can help to *normalize* because they convey the sense that others have had similar experiences of difficulty or trauma. This is particularly poignant for clients who are suffering the aftereffects of sexual abuse because they often feel unique and alone in their experience. Stories that normalize, but do not invalidate or downplay one's experiences, can help clients to feel a little less shameful and a little less isolated. Therapists can use stories as a way of acknowledging clients' experiences and letting them know that they have been heard.

Stories can also offer *hope.* One way this occurs is by highlighting alternate ways of viewing and doing things. Clients can get the sense that things can change, and there are possibilities in the future. Hope and an expectation of change are embedded in some stories.

There is a Hasidic story of a rabbi who was consulted by two men who are having a conflict. The rabbi listens to the first man, who advocates for his point of view in the matter. When the first man finishes, the rabbi declares, "You are right." The second man objects, and proceeds to relate his view. The rabbi says, "Yes, you are right." The rabbi's assistant, who has been listening, interjects, "Wait a minute, Rabbi, they can't both be right!" To this, the rabbi responds, "And you are right." Our view of stories is similar. There may not be any one correct meaning.

Take a moment to reflect on this question: In what way have the stories from the first six chapters of this book resonated with you or contributed to the creation of new meanings for you? Whatever meanings or understandings you have created from those stories are right. Stories can be somewhat specific in addressing certain aspects of clients' experiences, yet they must also be general enough that new meanings can arise. Although a meaning may be intended by the therapist, it is ultimately the meaning generated by the client that is right for him or her. Stories act as guideposts to the larger self—the inclusive self. They seem to go beyond the stuck self and tap into those resources that people have.

So, how do you remember, decide which ones to use, and recount stories? Most people remember stories by association. That is, when a person experiences something, it somehow resonates in such a way that it triggers a memory or previous experience. Thus, we are not just talking about stories in the literal sense. Stories can be a compilation of memories and experiences that have led to some sort of new meaning for the person. Bill has what he calls "file folder" of stories. It's a metaphor for having stories filed away within him. When he hears something from a client that resonates with him, he goes to that file folder. As a client talks about a problem, we become interested in stories that relate to the solving of the problem. Having studied with Milton Erickson, Bill noticed a particular way that Erickson went about telling stories. When Erickson would hear about a problem, he would typically tell stories with solutions in them. Bill has expanded on this way of storytelling and has deemed it "class of problems/class of solutions" (O'Hanlon, 1987).

For example, if a person is talking about self-criticism, the class of solution would be, What are the ways to not self-criticize? This might include being less self-conscious, so that one doesn't notice what one does in a critical way:

Bob worked with a young, male, trauma victim who had been so severely beaten that he almost died. Although he had resolved his fear of being subjected to another attack, he was extremely self-critical, continually telling himself that he wasn't good enough to play high school sports. He was an excellent athlete, but he had convinced himself that he wasn't "in the same league as the others." One of the stories Bob told the young man was about Michael Jordan. When Jordan first tried out for his high school basketball team, he failed to make it. He became extremely upset and self-critical. A coach at the high school had a sense that Michael could eventually make it, and told him that if he would come to the gym before school everyday he would work with him so he could make the team in the future. Of course, he made the team. Although he challenges himself to compete at the highest level, Michael Jordan is no longer self-critical.

After hearing this story, the young man said he would sometimes hear his father talking to others about how he loved to watch his son compete. The father told compelling stories that made the young man feel competent and confident in his abilities. He was asked how he might replay these stories that were supportive to him. The young man replied that all he had to do was think of his father and that would trigger the supportive memories. He returned to team sports two months later.

Different stories resonate with people in differing ways. Interestingly, the stories that we believe are the most profound often seem to have little impact on clients. Conversely, the stories that we think are simple and unsensational can have deep effects. Clients will come back months later and say, "That story you told me about the boat, that really made a difference for me!" And we will be struggling to remember the story. Stories reach clients at different levels of experience. So what we want to do is pay attention to the verbal and nonverbal responses of clients to stories. Their responses inform us as to how to proceed.

CHANGING THE CONTEXT

In changing the context, we examine the person's:

❖ History.

❖ Culture/subculture.

❖ Genetic/biochemical background.

❖ Family background.

❖ Gender training.

❖ Spatial patterns.

❖ Time patterns.

By systematically examining those aspects of the context, we try to isolate the facets that create or support the problem.

We also seek to identify recessed aspects that might be brought to the foreground to help solve the problem:

Bill worked with Nancy—a woman in a bad marriage. Nancy's husband was very critical and sarcastic. He berated her for having gained weight. He mocked her feminist views and friends, telling her things like, "If your bra-burning friends could see what a wimp you are here at home, they'd lose all respect for you."

In addition to stress at home, Nancy had problems at work. She worked in a high-pressure job with a lot of office politics.

When Nancy's husband left her for a younger woman, she was devastated. Her friends, however, thought she was better off and gave her a party. As she got more distance from the breakup, she started to see that it was for the best that they had broken up. But a strange thing began happening at work. She started to doubt her competence and question her own decisions. Her doubts undermined her work performance, and her position became precarious. She returned to see Bill and asked for help.

Bill listened as Nancy explained that she thought that the messages she got from her father about the inadequacy of females in general and her in particular, combined with her ex-husband's and society's negative messages about women, were coming to haunt her. She said they were like tapes playing in her head all the time, undermining her. Bill agreed, but pointed out that Nancy must have some alternative messages because she had been able to function very effectively on the job despite those messages all these years. What were those alternative tapes? She immediately got a big smile on her face and said: "Margaret Mead and Eleanor Roosevelt." These women were her role models when she was coming of age, Nancy realized she had tapes from those heroines as well as the negative tapes from her father and ex-husband. She and

Bill spent the rest of the time talking about how she could turn up the volume on the Margaret Mead/Eleanor Roosevelt messages and turn down the father/ex-husband tapes.

So, while parts of the context may contribute to or add to the problem, there are usually other parts of the context that can provide solutions.

Another way to use the context to solve problems is to use the information not as a deterministic explanation, but as a way to normalize. "Of course, given that you were raised in a family that had a tradition of drinking or using medications to cope with difficulties, it is understandable that you are feeling like drinking when you are facing this challenge in your life." Or, "The German way is to just push through and not let your feelings bother you, so when you get into a hassle with your partner, your tendency is to get very rational. But that gets her more discouraged about the relationship and wants to leave. So you are seeing that it doesn't get you what you want, even though that is your first impulse."

Again, our job is to move the person from stuckness to possibility. We usually do this by validating and valuing the person, acknowledging the problematic aspects of the situation, and then evoking the solution aspects that have often been recessed or unrecognized.

SUMMARY POINTS
CHAPTER SIX

❖ This model holds that there are four areas for intervention in therapy with people who have been abused: Experience, Actions, Stories, and Context.

❖ After acknowledging experience, it's important to help people change their actions (see Chapter Three). This chapter details how to help people change the problematic stories that support the problem.

❖ People who have been abused develop four problematic stories about themselves or their situations:

1. Stories that blame.

2. Stories that invalidate or suggest that the person's experience is wrong or untrustworthy.

3. Stories that imply that a person has no choice or responsibility for the actions they take.

4. Stories that suggest that change is impossible.

❖ People also develop identity stories that don't fully represent them or that represent them in an unfavorable light.

❖ Therapy can help resurrect or create alternative stories that enable people to resolve their problems.

CHAPTER SEVEN

*Weaving New
Webs and Breaking
Old Ones*

CONTINUITY AND TRANSITION
RITUALS FOR HEALING

*S*UE DIDN'T REALLY LIKE *her life. She was single and lonely, unhappy in her job. She had health problems and was overweight. She had been sexually abused as a child, and she never felt as if she was really lovable. One day, at the supermarket, a man approached her and started a conversation. He asked her about how to cook squash. She politely answered his query and moved on. The man casually followed her through the store. At first she was a bit annoyed and scared, but he was so charming that after a while, Sue spoke to him. Near the end of the shopping trip, Jack formally introduced himself and asked Sue to go out with him. Flattered, she agreed, still not sure of him, but intrigued and excited. Perhaps her life would take a turn for the better, she thought.*

The next few months were blissful. Jack turned out to be quite romantic, bringing her flowers, calling daily, writing her love poems. He was a successful businessperson who made over $100,000 per year, he told her. They ended up falling in love and soon were having sex.

Then, a few troubling signs began to surface. Jack refused to give Sue his home phone number or his address. He told her that he liked his privacy, and if she needed to call, she could call him on his cellular phone, which he kept in his truck. He started telling her his fantasies about having sex with her and another woman. He lied about little things on occasion. Still, aside from these minor complaints, the relationship was going well. Sue was happy for the first time in her life. Friends and coworkers told her that she was blossoming. She began to talk to Jack about getting married and he seemed eager at the prospect.

One day, Sue happened to mention Jack's name to a neighbor who, in their casual conversation, asked if Jack's wife still worked at the telemarketing firm. Sue was stunned and thought the neighbor must have gotten Jack confused with someone else. But when she investigated, she found out that Jack was indeed married and even had a teenage son. When she confronted Jack with her discoveries, he became enraged at her "snooping." Later, he came to her house, confronted her, and, when she stood her ground, raped her anally. She never saw him again.

When Sue sought therapy, she was still upset and unfinished about the situation she had gotten herself into with Jack. She avoided people and was fearful of any man who showed an interest in her. She felt dirty, she said, especially her hair. Jack had admired her red hair and had once given her a very sensual shampoo. In discussing the situation, the song from the musical South Pacific *came to mind: "I'm Gonna Wash That Man Right Outta My Hair." With that start, Sue designed a ceremony in which she wrote Jack and her father (who had abused her in childhood) letters that expressed all her feelings of being deceived, violated, and abandoned. She then burned the letters and washed her hair over and over again, listening to the song, until she felt she had washed Jack and her father right out of her life.*

CONTINUITY AND STABILITY RITUALS
RECLAIMING WHAT THE ABUSE STOLE

Steve and Sybil Wolin (1993) conducted research on the resiliency of children from dysfunctional families. These were children from alcoholic and abusive families. Steve and Sybil wondered, why don't all children who were raised in alcoholic families turn out alcoholic or with the classic, Adult Children of Alcoholics (ACoA) syndrome? Some do, but many don't. They were interested in the exceptions.

One of their key discoveries from research was that children did not develop as many dysfunctional patterns in adulthood if there seemed to have been no disruption in the family rituals. Everyday routines and activities remained a constant in these children's lives. We are both from large families where everyone would gather together at the same time for dinner each evening. Although things may have been chaotic with lots of kids running around and many different activities going on simultaneously, everyone knew that dinner was at the same time each night. It was a stable activity in our everyday lives.

Along with the daily dinners, we had other daily, weekly, monthly, seasonal, and annual rituals. These regular activities helped us connect with ourselves and inoculate us from some of the troubles that can plague children from dysfunctional homes. The Wolins found that children whose rituals were disrupted didn't do as well.

Part of what we can do with people who have been abused, then, is to help them restore old habits that have been disrupted by their traumas, or help them create new ones. We refer to these as rituals of *continuity* or *stability*. These are habits that help establish some stability or connection to themselves or others in their lives.

Any disruption or trauma can disconnect people from their rituals of stability or connection. This disruption does not have to be something such as a death or an illness. It could be a desirable event, such as the birth of a child or the changing of a job. Say a married couple had a ritual of going to dinner together once a week to talk. Then they have a baby and they find that they no longer are spending the time together that they used to. They lose the ritual of connecting. Or, it could be that before the birth of her baby, the wife had time to sit and think. That changed with the arrival of her child. In terms of change—positive or negative—it is particularly important to maintain old stability rituals or create new ones. Stability rituals can be ones that connect one to others or one to oneself:

Bill had a client, Marcia, who had been abused. As an adult, Marcia had created the ritual of locking the door to her house and the door to her bedroom every night, which made her feel extra safe. She would also hold a teddy bear, light incense, listen to new age music, and drink herbal bedtime tea. The ritual engaged all the senses. Marcia would then write in her journal, sort of a message from herself to herself, to connect her with what she had experienced that day. After doing this ritual for awhile, anytime Marcia began to feel disconnected, all she would have to do is put on the music or light the incense and she would be reminded to reconnect.

Steve Gilligan (personal communication, 1992) has this idea that when organisms are traumatized, they naturally

TABLE 7.1
CONNECTIVE/STABILITY RITUALS:
REGULARLY REPEATED ACTIVITIES
Activities Clients Can Count On.   Daily; seasonal; holidays.
Continuity Rituals.   Restoring previous rituals.
Connecting Rituals.   Prescribing a ritual that restores or makes connections to people or situations.
Rituals of Remembering.   Rituals that help connect with memories, the past, and disconnected resources.
Rites of Inclusion.   Designed to make people part of a social group or relationship.

withdraw. If a dog has been hit by a car on the highway, but not killed, it might well attempt to move away from or snap at the proffered hand of a passing stranger. People respond by withdrawing, too. When traumatized, they withdraw from aspects of themselves or others and sometimes they don't reconnect. Our job, as therapists, is to help them to reconnect to themselves or to others.

Anthropology is rife with descriptions of the kinds of rituals people do to connect and stabilize their lives. Table 7.1 summarizes some of the connection and stability rituals that we have used to help people reconnect.

TRANSITION RITUALS: LEAVING OLD
ROLES AND PAIN BEHIND

The second kind of ritual that we use in treating clients who are suffering the aftereffects of sexual abuse is a *transition ritual*. Transition rituals are helpful when people have an identity story or unfinished business that they need to leave behind. A transition ritual offers these people a very physical, action-based way to disrupt the old story and move to a new story, or sense of themselves. Transition rituals include rites of passage, rites of mourning, and rites of exclusion (see Table 7.2). To do this kind of ritual, we help people find symbols. A symbol is usually something that concretizes and externally represents the unfinished experience within the person. Symbols should be physical objects that can be carried around, burned, or buried:

In the context of family therapy, Bob worked with Laurie, a young woman who would self-mutilate by putting burn marks on her legs with a lighter. Laurie said that the black burn marks

TABLE 7.2
TRANSITION RITUALS

Special Activities Marked Out from Everyday Life.   Special time(s), place(s), clothing, foods, scents, activities; restricted to special people.

Rites of Passage.   Designed to move people from one role or developmental phase to another and to have that validated and recognized by others in their social context.

Rites of Exclusion.   Designed to eject or bar people from a social group or relationship.

Rites of Mourning/Leaving Behind.   Designed to facilitate or make concrete the end of some relationship or connection.

represented all the darkness in the world. She was an artistic young woman and very poetic in her description of things. Although she was not suicidal, her persistent self-mutilation was beginning to create scars and present medical problems because her wounds didn't always heal completely before she burned her legs again. Prior to Laurie's first appointment with Bob, her father, a pediatrician, had had his daughter hospitalized four times in six months for the self-mutilating behavior. After establishing an agreement with Laurie to not self-mutilate, Bob asked her if she felt that all the darkness and blackness the world had shown her was all that was there. She said that there were other colors too, but that black was mainly what she saw. Since she enjoyed painting, Bob suggested that the next time she felt the impulse to burn her legs, she work to capture the color she was trying to describe on canvas. The first of the young woman's paintings were very dark black with specks of gray and white. She said that those specks represented "the light that sometimes shows through

*the black." Her paintings gradually became lighter in shade
with less and less black present. She abandoned the self-
mutilating behavior and began to paint pictures of nature settings for other people. During the final therapy session, Laurie
said, "I can still see the light even if there's darkness."*

The painting served as a symbol for Laurie—she manipu-
lated the paint on the canvas instead of mutilating her legs.
In so doing, she was able to make the transition from darkness to light.

Symbols can help people recognize and express what they
are experiencing without doing it on their bodies or without
getting stuck in their bodies. When we do symbolic work, we
usually ask clients what symbol they think will work for them,
but we will also offer possibilities that others have used.
These include using a picture, a doll, a plant, a rock, and so
on. We've found that most people will choose, as at least part
of their ritual, to write something, but it really depends on the
person. Interestingly, a meta-analysis of 13 studies done by
Joshua Smyth of SUNY, Stonybrook, shows that writing, even
for only 20 minutes per day for as little as three days, about
traumatic events in one's life has positive effects on immune
system functioning and reported illness, as well as decreasing
work absenteeism and improving grades for students (reported in *USA Today,* April 1, 1996).

PHASES OF CREATING RITUALS

We use several steps to create a healing ritual:

1. *Introduce the idea of a ritual.* Clarify the purpose of
   the ritual and identify what is still unfinished for the

client. Brainstorm on what kind of symbol might be used for the ritual.

2. *Prepare the client to do the ritual.* Do not attempt a ritual before the client is emotionally and psychologically ready. The client needs to decide whether to do the ritual alone or involve a family member, friend, the therapist, or someone else.

3. *Do the ritual.*

4. *Create a respite experience.* There is usually a transition from doing the ritual back into everyday life. The person goes away from the ritual and does something else. This can be a kind of getaway that includes, but is not limited to, meditation or praying.

5. *Celebrate or reintegrate back into everyday life.* The final step in the ritual process can be a celebration—something that symbolizes that the person has moved on and has entered a new phase in life.

Some rituals combine both the transition and continuity. Having clients choose both *problem symbols* that they are going to leave behind and *solution* or *resource symbols* they are going to carry with them is a way of combining both.

Rituals give people something to *do* about the unfinished or disconnected feelings they have inside. Or to reconnect with their social environment after they have been cut off or disconnected by trauma.

In Chapter Eight, we will expand on the use of rituals, as well as add other ideas for dealing with the challenging and dangerous habit of self-mutilation. We will also discuss flashbacks and other troubling intrusions from the past.

SUMMARY POINTS
CHAPTER SEVEN

❖ Two kinds of rituals can be helpful for people who have been abused:

1. Stability rituals are used to help people recreate or create habits of connecting with themselves or others.

2. Transition rituals are used to help people move on from unfinished business or old stories that no longer fit.

❖ Some rituals require symbols—concrete, physical objects that represent either the problem or the solution.

CHAPTER EIGHT

A Safety Net

Innovative Methods for
Stopping Self-Harm and
Intrusive Flashbacks

*B*ILL HAD A CLIENT, *Jane, who, prior to coming to see him, developed a habit of cutting herself with razor blades. Jane was not suicidal. She would frequently show up bleeding at the emergency room, where they would fix her wounds and give her a lecture. She would go home and soon repeat the whole process.*

Because Jane lived a long way away, Bill saw her every two months for a long session. Bill told her that he really needed for her to stop the cutting because he would feel too constrained in the therapy, fearing to bring up tough subjects or get her to buckle down and do the hard work necessary because he would be afraid she would hurt herself in between sessions. Jane told him about an agreement she had once made with another therapist:

> *I agree not to hurt myself or anybody else, inside or out, by accident or on purpose, except if there's a reason to defend myself in the present reality, and if then, I can make a choice about how I respond, at least until I see you in person in your office next time.*

Bill told her that if she felt that she could not keep the agreement, she was to call him and talk to him before she hurt herself. After some time in treatment, she called him and said, "I'm feeling a great urge to cut myself. I don't think I can stop myself, and I promised you I'd call." Bill worked with the woman over the phone, and she promised to wait until they could meet again in two weeks. However, she was sure that she could not keep the agreement any longer than two weeks and wasn't sure she could renew it at the next session.

In the meantime, Bill had been out to a shopping mall where an antique show was going on. At this show, he came across a Raggedy Ann doll. Remembering an idea he had heard from Finnish psychotherapist Tapani Ahola, who had used a doll as a ritual device, Bill bought the doll. It was an old doll, from about 50 years ago and it didn't have an outfit on. The Raggedy Ann doll wore only a heart that said, "I love you." This spoke to many of Jane's issues.

When the woman came to her next session, Bill talked with her about having the urge to hurt herself. He then showed her the doll and said, "I bought this to take care of it." She looked at the doll and replied, "What's that?" Bill said, "This is you. The next time you feel the urge to hurt yourself and you don't think you can stop yourself, cut this doll instead." He also told her that if she cut the doll she would have to sew it back up. Jane could hardly look at the doll at first. She said, "I had a doll like that when I was younger and I used to make diapers out of the cloth napkins we had on our table." Bill replied, "I don't have any cloth napkins, but I have Kleenex." She made diapers for the doll out of Kleenex and Scotch tape. Then she could look at the doll and she took it home.

When she brought the doll back to the next session, Bill saw that Jane had cut the doll through the midsection gutting it, had cut through the throat, and had cut off the hands and feet. She was in a rage when she did this. She told Bill that this was what the people who abused her had threatened to do to her if she ever told anyone about the abuse. Following this, she sewed the doll back up and made coverings for all the scars. She then made a long dress for the doll, which also covered the cuts. Interestingly, after she sewed it up, the doll became her symbol of comfort and security. It helped her to feel connected and safe.

WHAT IS CUTTING AND SELF-HARM ABOUT?

In Chapter Seven, we gave some examples of self-mutilation and ways of using rituals with harmful actions to self, but the question remains: What is the phenomenon of cutting and self-harm all about? Our answer is that self-harm has numerous aspects and explanations. We have learned to merely investigate the inner experience and explanations that a particular client has, because he or she can educate us about what it means and what it does for him or her. We have, however, found some common themes regarding self-harm.

As discussed in Chapter One, people often dissociate when traumatized as a means to cope with an untenable and overwhelming situation. Later, however, they use this coping mechanism to deal with situations that they have inaccurately perceived as harmful. So this automatic dissociation is an unconscious process and sometimes occurs out of context. Bill has this saying, "The unconscious mind is sometimes smart about things it's dumb to be smart about." When the context is changed and the person is in a safe place, with a safe person, they dissociate inappropriately and unnecessarily because the unconscious doesn't distinguish between the traumatic context and the safe context. So sometimes the self-harming behavior is a way to dissociate from the current context:

Bob met with Janine, a young woman who would find herself "mindlessly" digging her fingernails into her left arm whenever she was in a room without windows. During her abuse, which had been in a walk-in closet, she had dissociated to escape the pain, but now the context was different and the unwanted dissociative action was repeating itself.

We have learned from our clients that there are also situations in which self-harming behavior is a re-creation of previous bad feelings, an escape from other feelings (either painful or pleasurable), a way to relieve internal pressure, as an anesthesia or numbing technique, and a way to reconnect with the body. These experiences are all reflections of a quotation (by Émile Chartier) we came across, "There is nothing as dangerous as an idea when it's the only one you have." People who are self-harming are often stuck (frozen in time) with only one way to cope. By exploring a particular way of coping that usually doesn't work to resolve the problem or creates more problems, we can determine the best way to disrupt and stop the harmful behavior.

PRACTICAL TECHNIQUES FOR REDUCING
OR ELIMINATING CUTTING/SELF-HARM

The main methods we have for reducing or eliminating cutting and self-harm, besides those already detailed in previous chapters, fall into two categories: (a) finding at least one alternative to accomplish the same end that the self-harm used to accomplish and (b) reorienting the person to the present context:

A woman who used cutting to relieve pressure she felt building up inside was asked about other ways of relieving pressure. She came up with several things she might do to handle or relieve pressure: She could do something productive, she could do some relaxation techniques or meditation, she could call a friend, or she could get a facial and have her nails done. She agreed to try one of the things on her list before she cut herself the next time. She found that she didn't need to cut when she used other methods of relieving pressure.

We also use methods to both reorient people to the present reality and to connect with their resources:

For the woman mentioned earlier, who was digging her nails into her skin, Bob suggested that she select a small item that she could keep with her and that symbolized safety for her. She chose a tennis bracelet with three hearts on it that she had just received as a present. She then began to wear it on her left wrist. When she would go into rooms without windows or near closed spaces such as elevators, she would touch the bracelet or hold her left wrist so she could feel it. Since the bracelet represented love and safety and she knew that she had received the bracelet long after the abuse, it helped her to stay in the present time and present place so she didn't dissociate and do the self-harming action.

PRACTICAL TECHNIQUES FOR REDUCING OR ELIMINATING INTRUSIVE FLASHBACKS

Like self-harm, flashbacks often call the person from the present to a past context. So, our main approach with flashbacks is to wake people from the symptomatic trance and orient them to the current context and reality. We heard that a psychiatrist from Menninger Clinic in Topeka, Kansas, recommended a simple procedure to use with patients who hallucinate in the therapist's office. He suggested that the therapist have the patient touch the desk, and pay close attention to the physical feeling of the desk. Why? To bring the person out of that internal focus back to the present

reality. It is much the same with flashbacks. We suggest to
people that they begin to reorient to the present sensory reality when in the midst of flashbacks:

*A couple was having sexual difficulties because she would
flashback to her sexual abuse by her father while the couple
was having sex. A simple intervention helped reduce the
flashbacks. If she began to have them, they should halt the
sexual interaction and she should deliberately look at her
husband's face, touch his face, look at his body, and have
him talk to her. This had the effect of bringing her out of the
flashbacks and into the current reality. This wasn't her father who was abusing her and wanted to get his pleasure
from her. This was her husband who loved her and wanted
to share pleasure with her.*

GET AGREEMENTS FOR SAFETY AND
SECURITY IF NECESSARY

We have discussed the distinction between people's internal
experiences and their actions. To reiterate, all internal experiences are okay, whereas some actions are okay and some
are not. Actions that include harm to self or others are never
okay. Although people who self-mutilate are often not suicidal, we want to intervene when any type of self-harming
action is occurring with clients. Thus, agreements for safety
and security are sometimes necessary.

There are several ways to get these agreements. In some
instances, verbal agreements work well. Bill's case example at
the beginning of this chapter provides a way of framing an
agreement for nonharmful action. Our understanding is that
a form of this contract initially came from Bennett Braun, a
psychiatrist in the Chicago area:

I agree not to hurt myself or anybody else, by accident or on purpose, except if there's a reason to defend myself in the present reality, and if then, I can make a choice about how I respond, at least until I see you in person in your office next time.

This type of agreement can also be modified to include contacting and talking with a psychiatrist or other mental health professional, going to the emergency room, or some other method of alerting others of the situation before doing anything harmful to oneself or others.

For other clients, it may be necessary to have a written contract because verbal agreements sometimes are not enough. Written contracts also symbolize different things for clients. Such contracts should be specific to each client as some people have had experiences of breaking written agreements, while others treat them very seriously.

In some cases, it may be necessary to have another person or persons involved who can help with the carrying out of a safety plan. Family therapists Cloé Madanes (1981, 1990) and Jay Haley (1987, 1996) have made frequent use of "suicide watches." This involves mobilizing family and friends of the suicidal person and having them keep a watch on the person 24 hours a day until the threat of suicide is diminished or gone. This usually bypasses the hospitalization process and also puts pressure on the person to resolve the suicidal issues more quickly.

It's important not to get too pushy or rigid with these contracts. Again, our message is to treat each situation as unique and individualize your approach:

Bill worked with a client who had been abused. She had been referred by a psychologist who, once he had heard she had considered killing herself, insisted that she make a contract for safety with him. She was reluctant, but he was adamant that he couldn't work with her if she would not ensure her safety. She made the contract and instantly became compulsively suicidal. It took every ounce of her will not to act on the impulse. She finally decided to stop treatment with him. When she came to see Bill, she told him that she thought the contract was only to protect the psychologist legally and that she had been suicidal for years without ever acting on it. So, Bill agreed to work with her without a contract. They were able to complete their work with no more trouble with the suicidal impulses.

Summary Points
Chapter Eight

❖ Many dynamics are involved in cutting or self-harming behavior. It is unwise to assume one knows what the behavior is about; instead, ask clients what they experience or how they explain it to themselves.

❖ We typically use two methods for reducing or eliminating self-harming behavior:

1. Find at least one alternative that satisfies the same need or intention that the self-harming behavior does and encourage use of the alternative.

2. Help reorient clients to the present context by having them pay attention to current sensory experience, thereby bringing them out of their "symptomatic trance."

❖ We also use the method of reorienting people to the present reality to help bring them out of their absorption in flashbacks.

❖ It may be necessary to get an agreement from the person for safety in cases of extreme suicidality, homicidality, and self-harm. Make sure to close all the potential loopholes in the agreement.

Envoi

Embrace Your Deviance
and Double
Your Weirdness

The Irish Potato Famine was brought about because tenant farmers in Ireland, struggling to get the highest price for their crops, began to specialize in the best cash crop of the time, potatoes. In 1845 and 1846 when a potato rust infested the crops and caused them to fail, it cut a swath right through the Irish land and economy. Many thousands of people died as a result. Biologists and agricultural scientists know the dangers confronting an organism that has only one strain—it leaves the entire species in jeopardy.

We have written this book to provide another strain to the dominant species of sexual abuse trauma treatment. Psychotherapy, unlike sociology and psychology, which deal in statistics and groups, always works with an N of 1. Therefore, even the ideas in this book should be held very lightly and never put above the unique needs of the particular client. We don't always follow these methods when we work with people—but we almost always do. And we find this approach fits well for us and almost all the clients we see.

Bill was participating in a panel discussion at a large conference on sexual abuse. The topic was male sexual abuse, and after the rather theoretical and clinical discussions of the other panelists, Bill had his turn. Having the sense that the academic side of things was well covered already, Bill decided on a more personal presentation. He told the story of his abuse by his grandfather. Just before he began to speak, he noticed that his friend Stephen Gilligan, had walked into the room to listen to the presentation. Steve had never heard Bill speak about his abuse before. Bill told the story in both a poignant and a humorous way, as is his style, and participants found themselves both tearing up and laughing.

When it came time for audience comments and questions, Steve Gilligan stood up and said to everyone in the room: "I just want you all to know that Bill O'Hanlon is a deviant." People either gasped in horror that someone was saying this about Bill after he'd just been so open and vulnerable, or they laughed uncomfortably. But Steve continued, "No, I mean it. You heard Bill's presentation, the way he told it in his inimitable style. He's clearly a deviant. The impressive part is that he seems very comfortable with his deviance. He embraces his deviance. I think that can be an inspiration for us all." Bill knew that one of Steve's treasured principles of life is: "You are an incurable deviant, but then again so is everyone else," so he took this as a nice compliment. After that incident, Bill began to openly declare himself a "deviant and proud of it" on any occasion that warranted it.

Several months later, Bill was giving a keynote address at a psychotherapy conference. His talk, entitled "No Guru, No Method, No Teacher OR If You Meet Erickson on the Road, Kill Him!" was aimed at getting his listeners to find their own unique voices and styles as therapists. As part of the talk, he told the story of how he became a proud deviant with the help of his friend Steve Gilligan. After the talk, a woman came up and said she was moved to tell Bill a story because of his story about being a proud deviant. She had attended an eight-week class with a spiritual teacher from India on the advice of a friend of hers who had previously attended the series and had gotten a lot from it. She signed up for the class and she too enjoyed it, except that every week the teacher kept repeating a phrase that she found troubling and puzzling. He kept punctuating his lectures with the phrase: "You must double your weirdness!" He seemed so adamant about it that she tried to make sense of it, but remained stumped. Finally, after she had gotten used to his Indian accent, she realized that all along, he had really been saying,

"You must develop your awareness!" She had felt rather foolish after her realization, until she heard Bill's speech and Bill's story about deviance. Perhaps the more profound spiritual message and quest was to double her weirdness rather than to develop her awareness.

We sincerely hope that this book has helped you to proudly embrace your deviance and your uniqueness, and double your weirdness. And maybe even double your success when doing this important work with people who have been abused.

REFERENCES

Aldridge-Morris, R. (1989). *Multiple personality: An exercise in deception.* London: Erlbaum.

American Psychiatric Association. (1994). *Diagnostic and statistical manual of mental disorders* (4th ed.). Washington, DC: American Psychiatric Association.

Araoz, D. L. (1985). *The new hypnosis.* New York: Brunner/Mazel.

Bateson, G. (1972). *Steps to an ecology of mind: A revolutionary approach to man's understanding himself.* New York: Ballantine Books.

Chopra, D. (1989). *Quantum healing: Exploring the frontiers of mind/body medicine.* New York: Bantam Books.

Coons, P. M. (1986). The prevalence of multiple personality disorder. *Newsletter of the International Society for the Study of Multiple Personality and Dissociative Disorders, 4,* 6–7.

de Shazer, S. (1988). *Investigating solutions in brief therapy.* New York: Norton.

Dolan, Y. M. (1991). *Resolving sexual abuse: Solution-focused therapy and Ericksonian hypnosis for adult survivors.* New York: Norton.

Erickson, M. H. (1954). Pseudo-orientation in time as a hypnotherapeutic procedure. *Journal of Clinical and Experimental Hypnosis, 2,* 261–283.

179

Gilligan, S. G. (1987). *Therapeutic trances: The cooperation principle in Ericksonian hypnosis.* New York: Brunner/Mazel.

Gruber, H., & Voneche, J. (1977). *The essential Piaget.* New York: Basic Books.

Haley, J. (1987). *Problem solving therapy* (2nd ed.). San Francisco: Jossey-Bass.

Haley, J. (1996). *Learning and teaching therapy.* New York: Guilford Press.

Herman, J. L. (1992). *Trauma and recovery: The aftermath of violence—from domestic abuse to political terror.* New York: Basic Books.

Hubble, M. A., & O'Hanlon, W. H. (1992). Theory countertransference. *Dulwich Centre Newsletter,* 25–30.

Hudson, P. O., & O'Hanlon, W. H. (1991). *Rewriting love stories: Brief marital therapy.* New York: Norton.

Kaminer, W. (1992). *I'm dysfunctional, you're dysfunctional.* Reading, MA: Addison-Wesley.

Kardiner, A., & Spiegel, H. (1947). *War, stress and neurotic illness* (Rev. ed.). New York: Hoeber.

Laing, R. D. (1967). *The politics of experience.* New York: Pantheon Books.

Le Guin, U. K. (1968). *A wizard of Earthsea.* New York: Bantam Books.

Lord, B. B. (1990). *Legacies: A Chinese mosaic.* New York: Fawcett Columbine.

Madanes, C. (1981). *Strategic family therapy.* San Francisco: Jossey-Bass.

Madanes, C. (1990). *Sex, love, and violence: Strategies for transformation.* New York: Norton.

North, C. S., Ryall, J. M., Ricci, D. A., & Wetzel, R. D. (1993). *Multiple personalities, multiple disorders: Psychiatric classification and media influence.* New York & Oxford, England: Oxford University Press.

O'Hanlon, B. (1982). Strategic pattern intervention: An integration of individual and family systems therapies based on the work of Milton H. Erickson, M.D. *Journal of Strategic and Systemic Therapies, 1*(4), 26–33.

O'Hanlon, B. (1993). Frozen in time: Possibility therapy with adults who were sexually abused as children. In L. VandeCreek, S. Knapp, & T. L. Jackson (Eds.), *Innovations in clinical practice* (Vol. 12). Sarasota, FL: Professional Resource Press.

O'Hanlon, B. (in press). Frozen in time: Possibility therapy with adults who were sexually abused as children. In S. O'Hanlon & B. Bertolino (Eds.), *Evolving possibilities: The selected papers of Bill O'Hanlon.* Santa Fe, NM: Possibility Press.

O'Hanlon, B., & Beadle, S. (1994). *A field guide to Possibility-Land: Possibility therapy methods.* Omaha, NE: Possibility Press.

O'Hanlon, B., & Hudson, P. (1996). *Love is a verb: How to stop analyzing your relationship and start making it great!* New York: Norton.

O'Hanlon, B., & Wilk, J. (1987). *Shifting contexts: The generation of effective psychotherapy.* New York: Guilford Press.

O'Hanlon, W. H. (1987). *Taproots: Underlying principles of Milton Erickson's therapy and hypnosis.* New York: Norton.

O'Hanlon, W. H., & Martin, M. (1992). *Solution-oriented hypnosis: An Ericksonian approach.* New York: Norton.

O'Hanlon, W. H., & Weiner-Davis, M. (1989). *In search of solutions: A new direction in psychotherapy.* New York: Norton.

Orne, M. (1959). The nature of hypnosis: Artifact and essence. *Journal of Abnormal Psychology, 58,* 277.

Parker, R. (1995). *Thin air.* New York: Putnam.

Putnam, F. W. (1986). The scientific investigation of multiple personality disorder. In J. M. Quen (Ed.), *Split minds/split brains: Historical and current perspectives* (pp. 109–125). New York: New York University Press.

Ritterman, M. (1983). *Using hypnosis in family therapy.* San Francisco: Jossey-Bass.

Ross, C. A. (1989). *Multiple personality: Diagnosis, clinical features, and treatment.* New York: Wiley.

Rossi, E. L. (1980). *The nature of hypnosis and suggestion: The collected papers of Milton H. Erickson on hypnosis* (Vol. 1). New York: Irvington.

Simon, R. (1982/1992). Behind the one-way mirror: An interview with Jay Haley. In R. Simon (Ed.), *One on one: Conversations with the shapers of family therapy* (pp. 1–18). Washington, DC: Family Therapy Network/New York: Guilford Press.

Taylor, W. S., & Martin, M. F. (1944). Multiple personality. *Journal of Abnormal Social Psychology, 39,* 281–300.

Thigpen, C. H., & Cleckley, H. M. (1984). On the incidence of multiple personality disorder: A brief communication. *International Journal of Clinical and Experimental Hypnosis, 32,* 63–66.

White, M., & Epston, D. (1990). *Narrative means to therapeutic ends.* New York: Norton.

Whyte, D. (1989). *Belonging to the world* [Audio cassette]. Langley, WA: Many Rivers.

Wolin, S. J., & Wolin, S. (1993). *The resilient self: How survivors of troubled families rise above adversity.* New York: Villard Books.

INDEX